Truth Springs from the Earth

Truth Springs from the Earth

The Teachings of Rabbi Menahem Mendel of Kotsk

Morris M. Faierstein

PICKWICK *Publications* · Eugene, Oregon

TRUTH SPRINGS FROM THE EARTH
The Teachings of Rabbi Menahem Mendel of Kotsk

Pickwick Publications
An Imprint of Wipf and Stock Publishers
199 W. 8th Ave., Suite 3
Eugene, OR 97401

www.wipfandstock.com

PAPERBACK ISBN: 978-1-5326-3725-4
HARDCOVER ISBN: 978-1-5326-3727-8
EBOOK ISBN: 978-1-5326-3726-1

Cataloguing-in-Publication data:

Names: Faierstein, Morris M., editor and author.

Title: Truth springs from the earth : the teachings of rabbi Menahem Mendel of Kotsk / Morris M. Faierstein.

Description: Eugene, OR: Pickwick Publications, 2018 | Includes bibliographical references.

Identifiers: ISBN 978-1-5326-3725-4 (paperback) | ISBN 978-1-5326-3727-8 (hardcover) | ISBN 978-1-5326-3726-1 (ebook)

Subjects: LCSH: Menaham Mendel, of Kotsk, 1787–1859 | Hasidim | Judaism—Doctrines

Classification: BM525 F254 2018 (print) | BM525 (ebook)

The English translation of Biblical passages is taken from The Tanakh: The Holy Scriptures by permission of the University of Nebraska Press © 1985 by the Jewish Publication Society, Philadelphia.

Manufactured in the U.S.A.   03/22/18

For Rabbi Alana, Leon, and Maiyan Suskin
In celebration of Maiyan's Bar Mitzvah

R. Menahem Mendel once asked R. Isaac Meir of Gur about the verse, *"truth springs from the earth"* [Ps 85:12]. What does one plant in the earth that truth should sprout from it? R. Isaac Meir answered him, if you bury falsehood, then the truth will sprout from the earth. [S.S.K. IV:102; E.E. No. 121]

It is not appropriate to say everything we think, nor is it appropriate to write down everything we say, nor print everything we write. [E.E. No. 989]

Contents

CONTENTS

Preface

Rabbi Menahem Mendel of Kotsk is one of the most interesting and challenging figures of Hasidism in the nineteenth century. His search for truth and battles against falsehood and spiritual compromise are the subject of many legends, hagiographical stories, and anecdotes. Though he was irascible and demanding, he inspired the loyalty of disciples who went on to become the dominant leaders of Hasidism in Poland from the middle of the nineteenth century to the destruction of Polish Jewry in the Holocaust.

The largest problem in writing about R. Menahem Mendel is that he left no surviving writings. There is a legend that he would write furiously all year trying to distill his teachings into the confines of a book. On the eve of Passover he would review what he had written in the past year, and always found it wanting. Mere words on paper were not able to encompass the ideas that he was endeavoring to express. He would then proceed to burn the manuscript along with the leavened products that were traditionally burned on the eve of Passover. As a result, there are no writings by R. Menahem Mendel, and everything that we know about him comes from secondary sources.

It was not unusual for hasidic masters not to write down their writings. In some cases, they may have kept notes or notebooks where they jotted down ideas and summaries of teachings. It was also common for hasidic masters not to publish the teachings attributed to them, but this was left to disciples or descendants. R. Menahem Mendel presents a special problem in this regard. His descendants and disciples moved away from the radicalism of his teachings and adopted more conventional and conservative theological positions. As a result, there was little incentive to preserve and publish whatever of his teachings that had been preserved. The few references to R. Menahem Mendel that are found in the writings of his disciples and descendants are primarily interpretations of Talmudic passages or other non-controversial matters. The one exception among R. Menahem Mendel's

disciples was R. Samuel of Shinove who did include a selection of R. Menahem Mendel's teachings in his book, *Ramataim Zofim*. Prof. Jacob Levinger
explored this subject in two important articles. The second part of the Introduction below discusses many of these questions in greater detail.

Despite the inherent difficulties, the story of R. Menahem Mendel
and his teachings has attracted the attention of anthologists of hasidic
teachings, historical novelists, and scholars. A number of Kotsker sayings
and teachings are found in several collections of hasidic teachings and hagiographical stories, published at the end of the nineteenth century or the
beginning of the twentieth. However, wider interest in Kotsk can be dated
to the period 1918–21. Two authors, J. L. Slotnick [also known as Yehuda
Elzet, or Avida], a scholar of folklore and an official of the Mizrachi po-
litical party in Poland, and Joseph Opatoshu, a novelist, wrote about Kotsk
in ways that brought Rabbi Menahem Mendel to the attention of a wider
audience, albeit in a negative light. Slotnick disseminated the story of the
so-called "Friday Night Incident", which is discussed below.

In 1921, Opatoshu published his most famous novel, *In Poilishe Velder*
[In Polish Woods]. It was the first volume of a trilogy describing Jewish life
in Poland from the aftermath of the Napoleonic Wars to the beginning of
the twentieth century. This novel was so popular that it was translated into
eight languages, including English, and was filmed in Poland. The premiere
in 1926 was the occasion of riots by Hasidim who objected to its negative
portrayal of Hasidism, and R. Menahem Mendel of Kotsk in particular. A
central theme of this novel was the decline of Jewish religious life in the
years leading to the Polish Revolt of 1863. The primary illustration of this
decline was the hasidic court of Kotsk during the period of R. Menahem
Mendel's seclusion (1839–59). The picture painted by Opatoshu was a court
full of impiety, heresy, and sexual intrigues that were meant to remind the
reader of the sexual escapades of Jacob Frank, the false Messiah, and his
followers in eighteenth-century Poland.

Both Slotnick and Opatoshu, each for their own reasons, were not particularly concerned with R. Menahem Mendel, but had their sights on the
spiritual heirs of the Kotsk school, the hasidic dynasties of Ger, Sochaczew,
and Alexander, who were the most influential hasidic dynasties in early
twentieth century Poland. Attacking and denigrating the figure of R. Menahem Mendel was an indirect way of attacking the influence of his disciples
and they dynasties they founded. My study of the so-called "Friday Night
Incident," the most famous legendary story about R. Menahem Mendel is

illustrative of the problems with many of the depictions of R. Menahem
Mendel and his teachings. This study is found in the Appendix below.

Members of the hasidic community responded to these attacks in different ways. In 1938, Phinehas Zelig Gliksman, a religious Jew who had
imbibed the canons of scholarly writing, published a monograph about
the Kotsker Rebbe that sought to defend his reputation and respond to his
detractors. It can be considered the first study of R. Menahem Mendel that
can be considered scholarly in that the author documents his assertions
with a scholarly apparatus of notes and sources. The same year, Israel Artan, a follower of the Gur Hasidic School, published an anthology of teachings attributed to R. Menahem Mendel, entitled *Emet ve-Emunah* [Truth
and Faith]. He writes in the introduction to the first edition that he was
encouraged to compile this work by the Rebbe of Gur.

The first influential work on Kotsk after the Holocaust was a Yiddish
novel by Menashe Unger, a Yiddish writer and journalist. His work, *Przysucha and Kotsk*, was published in Buenos Aires, 1949 in a series entitled
Polish Jewry, by the Central Organization of Polish Jews in Argentina. This
series was a memorial to the recently destroyed Polish Jewish civilization
and the volumes in this series included a variety of genres, novels, poems,
memoirs, etc. Unger's work was a historical novel that followed in the foot-
steps of Opatoshu's, *In Polish Woods*. In more recent years, the fact that it
was a not particularly accurate historical novel has been forgotten and it
has been treated as a historical source. Recently, it has been translated into
English with a scholarly Introduction.[1] There have been several "popular"
books on Kotsk published in Hebrew that are neither fish nor fowl. That is,
they are not novels, but are not serious scholarly works. They uncritically
rehash the stories and legends about R. Menahem Mendel and Kotsk, and
contribute nothing to advancing our understanding.

The two books on Kotsk by Abraham Joshua Heschel are the most
significant studies of R. Menahem Mendel and his teachings in the postwar
period. Both books were finished shortly before his death and published
posthumously. The better-known work is *A Passion for Truth*. It was published in English and written for a general audience. In many respects it
was a theological meditation on the influence of Kotsk on Heschel's life and
thought, and what Heschel saw as the relevance of R. Menahem Mendel
and his teachings for the modern world. It was based on the scholarly re-
searches of Heschel's other book, *Kotsk: In Gerangel far Emesdikeit* [Kotsk;

1. Unger, *Fire Burns in Kotsk*.

The Struggle for Integrity]. This two-volume work written in Yiddish un-fortunately remains untranslated. An English translation of this important work remains a desideratum.[2]

Heschel's method was the result of his long-term scholarly research into the literature of the Przysucha-Kotsk school and Hasidism more broadly, and his personal experience of Hasidism. He writes that during his childhood in Warsaw, he still had contact with old Hasidim who had travelled to Kotsk in their youth, and others who had heard about Kotsk directly from those who had directly experienced it. In a real sense, Heschel was the last living link to the lived traditions of Kotsk who wrote about these traditions in a serious scholarly manner. His insights have increased value because of this direct experience, since much of Kotsk was an oral tradition that was first committed to writing more than half a century after the death of R. Menahem Mendel.

My goal in this work is twofold. First, to present a biographical study of what is known about R. Menahem Mendel that is based on historical research, instead of rehashing myths, legends, and stories without regard to their historical veracity. Secondly, to collect and present those teach-ings by R. Menahem Mendel that are accessible to a broader audience and that do not require paragraphs or more of analysis and explanation for a one-line comment. I have endeavored to sort through the collections of hasidic sayings from the Przysucha-Kotsk school that are about R. Mena-hem Mendel, and equally importantly are plausibly consistent with what we know about his life and teachings.

I have not made any effort to synthesize R. Menahem Mendel's teach-ings into a coherent theological narrative. The attempts that have been made to do this usually end up telling us more about the ideas of the person doing the synthesis than about R. Menahem Mendel. Years ago, when I was a graduate student looking for a dissertation topic, a study of R. Menahem Mendel and his teachings was at the top of my list of possible topics. After much deliberation and discussion with teachers and colleagues, I came to the conclusion that a work of scholarly rigor was impossible, with the fragmentary nature of the materials available to those interested in this fas-cinating figure. In the end, I wrote my dissertation on one of R. Menahem Mendel's closest disciples, and an interesting and original thinker in his own right, R. Mordecai Joseph Leiner of Izbica.[3]

2. For a review of this work see, Faierstein, Review of *Kotsk*.

3. Published as Faierstein, *All is in the Hands of Heaven*, 1989 (Rev. ed., 2005).

My *havruta* (study partner and colleague), Rabbi Alana Suskin, joined me in reviewing primary sources as I prepared this work. Her assistance as colleague and audience for my ideas helped clarify many issues and lightened my burden in judging which teachings to include and which would be too esoteric for the intended audience.

Morris M. Faierstein
Rockville, Maryland

Abbreviations

[Books in Jewish order]

Bible

Gen	Genesis
Exod	Exodus
Lev	Leviticus
Num	Numbers
Deut	Deuteronomy
1–2 Kgs	1–2 Kings
Isa	Isaiah
Jer	Jeremiah
Hos	Hosea
Jonah	Jonah
Mic	Micah
Ps	Psalms
Prov	Proverbs
Job	Job
Eccl	Ecclesiastes
Esth	Esther
Dan	Daniel

m.	Mishnah
Avot	Avot
Menah.	Menahot

Talmud

b.	Babylonian
Ber.	Berakhot
Pesah.	Pesahim
Yoma	Yoma
Sukkah	Sukkah
Rosh Hash.	Rosh Hashanah
Meg.	Megillah
Moed Kat.	Moed Katan
Hag.	Hagigah
Ketub.	Ketubot
Sotah	Sotah
Ked.	Kedushin
B. Bat.	Baba Bathra
Mak.	Makkot
Avod. Zar.	Avodah Zara
Tem.	Temurah

Midrash

Mek.	Mekhilta
Gen. Rab.	Genesis Rabbah
Exod. Rab.	Exodus Rabbah
Lev. Rab.	Leviticus Rabbah
Song Rab.	Song of Songs Rabbah
Tanh.	Tanhuma

A. Primary sources

A.R.	*Abir ha-Ro'im.*
E.E.	*Emet ve-Emunah.*
L.A.	Levinger, "Authentic Sayings".
L.H.	*Likkutim Hadashim.* Warsaw, 1899; Ashdod, 2003.
L.T.	Levinger, "Teachings of the Rabbi of Kotsk".
N.H.	*Niflaot Hadashot.*
O.T.	*Ohel Torah.*
R.Z.	*Ramatai'im Zofim.*
S.S.K.	*Siah Sarfei Kodesh.*

I. Introduction

A. R. Menahem Mendel's Biography

FROM ITS VERY BEGINNINGS, Hasidism was a movement that attracted two very different groups of followers and taught two distinct doctrines. It was a populist movement that sought to address the needs of ordinary Jews and to bring some spiritual comfort and joy to their lives. At the same time, it was an elitist movement that sought to give spiritual direction to members of the religious elite of Jewish society. This duality was inherent in the personality and teachings of the founder of Hasidism, Israel Baal Shem Tov (Besht). He earned his living as an itinerant writer of amulets that warded off illness and demons and disseminated his ideas as a teller of stories for a popular audience. In the modern popular imagination he is seen as a populist leader who was concerned with the needs of ordinary people. This picture is accurate as far as it goes, but it neglects the other dimension of the Besht. He was also a teacher of sophisticated spiritual doctrines aimed at members of the religious elite that were far beyond the understanding of ordinary people. The Besht's dual message of compassion and support for ordinary people coupled with spiritual direction for the intellectual elite attracted important scholars and spiritual adepts, along with many simple Jews. This twofold approach continued to be the model for Hasidic leadership in the generations that followed.

His disciple, R. Dov Ber, the Maggid of Mezhirech, succeeded the Baal Shem Tov. The Maggid, as he was known, was very different from the Baal Shem Tov. He was a retiring scholar with weak health, who did not travel as the Besht had done, but attracted disciples to his community. The Maggid was also a great organizer and undertook the initiative to send his disciples to the diverse Jewish communities of Eastern Europe to disseminate the teachings of Hasidism and establish Hasidic communities. After the Maggid's death in 1772, there was never again a single leader of the Hasidic movement. Instead, his disciples became the leading spiritual leaders in their own region and continued the work of spreading Hasidism. The leading disciples of the Maggid who brought Hasidim to central Poland and Galicia were R. Elimelech of Lyzhansk and R. Samuel Shmelke of Nikolsburg. Like the Maggid they saw the attraction of disciples and grooming them to be future leaders as an important part of their spiritual task. Their disciples formed the fourth generation of Hasidic leaders. At the same time, they also developed the teachings of Hasidism in new and creative directions.

The Seer of Lublin

Hasidism became a mass movement in Poland under the leadership of R. Jacob Isaac Horowitz,[1] known as the Seer of Lublin.[2] A disciple of R. Elimelech of Lyzhansk and R. Samuel Shmelke Horowitz of Nikolsburg, who had introduced Hasidism to Poland in the early 1770's,[3] the Seer began to act as a *zaddiq* during the latter years of his teacher, R. Elimelech of Lyzhansk. R. Elimelech felt unable to meet both the needs of his community and his own personal spiritual needs in his latter years, so he transferred some of his responsibilities to his disciple.[4] R. Jacob Isaac eventually exceeded the mandate given to him by his mentor, which led to a certain amount of tension between the master and his disciple. The Seer remained the dominant Hasidic leader in Poland for thirty years, from 1785, when he began his leadership as a *zaddiq* until his death on the ninth of *Ab (Tisha B'Ab)*, 1815.[5]

1. There are two uncritical biographies of the Seer based on Hasidic sources: Bromberg, *Ha-Hoze mi-Lublin*, and Alfasi, *Ha-Hoze mi-Lublin*. More recent scholarly studies of his teachings include Elior, "Between Yesh and Ayin," 167–218; Sack, "Iyyun be-Torato shel ha-Hoze," 219–39; Piekarz, *Bein Ideologia le Meziut*, 130–42.

2. The title "Seer" was attached to him after his lifetime. For the various explanations of this name see, Assaf, "Veha-Mitnagedim Hitlozezu," 161 n. 1. He will be referred to by this title since this is how he became known in Hasidic and scholarly literature.

3. Though R. Elimelech and R. Samuel Shmelke introduced Hasidism to Poland, it was the activities of the Seer that firmly established Hasidism in Poland. The most important Hasidic dynasties in Poland and Galicia were founded by disciples of the Seer, See, Liberman, *Ohel RH'L*, 2:52–53. For the subsequent history of Hasidism in Poland see, Aescoli, *Ha-Hasidut be-Polin*. A more recent study is Dynner, *Men of Silk*.

4. Elior, "Between Yesh and Ayin," 396–97.

5. The events leading to the Seer's death are the subject of many Hasidic legends. See Assaf, "Veha-Mitnagedim Hitlozezu," 161–208.

The early doctrine of the *zaddiq*, particularly in the teachings of R. Dov Ber, the Maggid of Mezhirech, emphasized his role as a guide and mentor for a small circle of spiritual adepts. The Maggid and his School concentrated on the spiritual aspects of existence and rejected the physical and material aspects of life.[6]

The Seer, following the direction of his mentor, R. Elimelech of Lyzhansk, understood the role of the *zaddiq* differently and highlighted the *zaddiq's* role in providing for the material well being of his followers. Rachel Elior has summarized the Seer's perspective on the role of the *zaddiq*.

> The dialectical change brought about by the doctrine of the *Zaddik* may be characterized as follows: it was the departure from the view of *devekut* and unification with the divine *ayin* as ends in themselves—the direct outcome of self-abnegation and indifference towards material existence, towards a *devekut* which has the aim of drawing down material plenty and providing leadership for the world. This shift of mystical endeavor from the metaphysical to the earthly sphere is also a shift of emphasis from the single purpose of fusion with God (transformation of *ani* into *a[y]in*) to the complexity of simultaneous identification with the *ayin* and the *yesh*.[7]

The Seer's concept of "material *zaddiq*ism"[8] was based on the reciprocal relationship of the *zaddiq* and his followers (Hasidim). The *zaddiq* was responsible for insuring the material and physical well being of his followers, particularly in the central areas of "life, children and sustenance."[9] The *zaddiq* does this by being the channel which brings down the divine flow (*shefa*) which makes the existence of the world possible. In return the Hasid's responsibilities to the *zaddiq* include submitting to the authority of the *zaddiq* in all areas of life and supporting the *zaddiq* financially. The Hasid would not undertake any significant activity like marrying off his children or entering into business ventures without the blessing of the *zaddiq*, which would ensure the success of the undertaking. The Hasid would also turn to the *zaddiq* in times of distress, whether health issues, financial failures or family problems. In all cases, a donation (*pidyon*) would accompany

---

6. Elior, "Between Yesh and Ayin," 432–33.

7. Ibid., 418. *Ayin* (nothing) refers to the divine source of all being. *Yesh* (being) refers to the material world.

8. I take the term "material *zaddiq*ism" from Elior. See her discussion in "Between Yesh and Ayin," 425–55. See also, Sack, "Iyyun be-Torato shel ha-Hoze," 219–20.

9. b. *Moed Kat.* 28a.

the consultation with the *zaddiq*. Concerns about spiritual growth and religious practice receded into the background. The majority of the Seer's disciples who established Hasidic courts after his death followed the Seer's doctrine of material *zaddiqism*.

The Yehudi of Przysucha

Among those who came to Lublin were young men from wealthier families who were well educated and sought spiritual direction and intellectual nourishment. The Seer did not have the time to give them the intensive spiritual guidance they desired and he directed these young men to his important disciple, R. Jacob Isaac of Przysucha, who became known as the "Yehudi."[10] The Yehudi and the minority of the Seer's disciples who followed him created what was seen by many as a spiritual revolution in Hasidism.[11] The focus shifted from comforting the masses to nurturing an elite seeking spiritual direction. The Yehudi's teachings focused on four key points: a stress on Talmud study and the role of the scholar; opposition to the emphasis on miracle working; allowing for delay of the time of prayer—insisting that spiritual readiness is more important than the rules concerning the time of prayer; the importance of individualism—each person finding his own path in the service of God. This is the "conventional" view of the Przysucha School. M. Piekarsz has questioned this perspective and argued that the *zaddiq* also played the same central role that he did in the other contemporaneous Schools of Hasidism. People came to the *zaddqim* of the Przysucha-Kotsk School for material blessings like they did to other *zaddiqim*.[12] It may not have been their central self-perception as a religious leader, but it was an integral part of Hasidism at that time.

R. Menahem Mendel of Tomaszow

One of the young men who came to Lublin seeking spiritual enlightenment and became a disciple of the Yehudi was Menahem Mendel Morgenstern.

---

10. There are several theories about this name. The most common one is that he was given this name to distinguish him from the Seer, who had the same first name. The basic study of the Yehudi remains, Rabinowicz, *Rabbi Yaakov Yizhak mi-Przysucha*.

11. Aescoli, *Ha-Hasidut be-Polin*, 62–64.

12. Piekarsz, *Ha-Hanhagah ha-Hasidit*, 283–92. See also below section 63, which supports Piekarsz's argument.

He was born in 1787, in Goray, in the province of Lublin.[13] His father, Yehudah Leib, was one of the wealthiest and most distinguished members of the community. His mother also was descended from an important family.[14] After completing his elementary education in Goray, he went to Zamosc to study with the important scholar R. Joseph Hochgelernter.[15] During the period of the third partition of Poland, 1795–1809, the province of Lublin was part of Austria and the Austrian laws concerning the Jews were applied. One of these laws stipulated that Jews could not marry until they demonstrated a mastery of German and learned a profession. Menahem Mendel studied German and pharmacy in Lemberg.[16] Many years later he said that he learned the language, but made sure that it did not harm him spiritually.[17] Having fulfilled these requirements, he married at the age of twenty, in 1807. His new wife came from Tomaszow and they settled there after the wedding. As was customary, his father-in-law, a wealthy householder, gave him a significant dowry. Some of the money was used for living expenses so that Menahem Mendel could continue his Talmudic studies and the rest was invested in a hide and leather business with a partner, but the business was not successful.[18]

Menahem Mendel's father, Yehudah Leib, was an opponent of Hasidism, even though his grandfather, David Halperin had been a disciple of the Baal Shem Tov.[19] Menahem Mendel made his first journey to the Seer of Lublin after his marriage and settlement in Tomaszow.[20] His father was very unhappy with this decision, but Menahem Mendel ignored his father's protestations.[21] Menahem Mendel explained his attraction to Hasidism in later years. He said that he had heard stories of the *zaddiqim* from an old Hasid. "He told and I heard."[22] When he came to Lublin, the Seer treated him with

---

13. This is the same town immortalized by Singer, *Satan in Goray*.

14. For more information on his distinguished ancestry, see Gliksman, *Der Kotsker Rebbe*, 7–10.

15. S.S.K. I:59. He was the author of *Sefer Mishnat Hakhamim* (Lemberg, 1792).

16. Gliksman, *Der Kotsker Rebbe*, 11–12.

17. See below, Saying 36, I.

18. S.S.K. I:59.

19. Gliksman, *Der Kotsker Rebbe*, 7–8.

20. Ibid., 12–13.

21. Heschel, *Kotsk*, I:275–76.

22. See below, Sayings, 36, A.

great respect and honored him.[23] Nonetheless, he was not comfortable with the Seer's teachings and was drawn to the Yehudi and his elitist approach, becoming a devoted disciple of the Yehudi.

Przysucha and the Opposition to Its Program

The Yehudi's elitist program aroused much opposition from both his teacher, the Seer, and many of his fellow disciples in Lublin. R. Uri of Strelisk, one of the Seer's disciples, verbalized the deeper dispute. He said:

> The Holy Yehudi wants to follow a new path in Hasidism, from top to bottom, to inflame the children of Israel that they should serve God with Torah and prayer together, and such a path has never been followed before.[24]

The breach between the Yehudi and his teacher also carried over to their respective disciples and supporters. It was a dispute between two very different perspectives on Hasidism which continued for many years. For example, each group had different views concerning the place of miracles and their relation to the role of the *zaddiq*. The Seer and his followers felt that the performance of miracles was one of the central validations of the *zaddiq* and one of his primary functions.[25] The Yehudi, on the other hand, scoffed at miracles. He is reported to have said: "It is no trick to be a miracle worker. Any Jew who has attained a level of spirituality can overturn heaven and earth. But to be a Jew [a *Yid*] is difficult."[26]

After Napoleon's invasion of Russia in 1812, which many saw as the biblically prophesied war of Gog and Magog, the Seer and many of his disciples attempted to bring the Messiah by theurgic means.[27] The Yehudi was among those who opposed this attempt, and his stand on this issue precipitated the final break between him and the Seer of Lublin. The Yehudi died several months after his departure from Lublin. His son Yerahmiel tried to succeed him, but he was a *zaddiq* more in the mold of the Seer, interested

---

23. See below, Sayings, 28, A.

24. Alfasi, *Ha-Hoze mi-Lublin*, 91.

25. On the centrality of miracles in the teachings of the Seer and his other disciples, see Rabinowicz, *Rabbi Yaakov Yizhak*, chapter 7.

26. Ibid., 97.

27. This episode is described in Buber, *For the Sake of Heaven*. On this literary and historical aspects of this work see, Werses, "Ha-Hasidut be-Aspeklaria Belletritist," 317–56; Shapira, "Shtei Darkei Geulah," 429–46.

in material *zaddiqism* and not an intellectual and spiritual mentor, like his father.[28] As a result, the majority of the Yehudi's intellectually oriented followers invested leadership of the group in the Yehudi's outstanding disciple, R. Simhah Bunem of Przysucha.[29]

R. Simhah Bunem of Przysucha

R. Simhah Bunem had an unusual background for a Hasidic *rebbe*.[30] His father, a wandering preacher, had originally come from Germany and spoke German. R. Simhah Bunem used his knowledge of German to advantage and spent a number of years working as a lumber merchant, traveling to Danzig and other large cities. When he decided to settle down, he qualified as a pharmacist and earned his living in this way for many years until he succeeded the Yehudi as the leader of the Przysucha School. His enemies argued that the secular world had tainted him, and they questioned his ability to be a Hasidic *rebbe*. R. Simhah Bunem's disciples rejected these accusations completely. They countered that although R. Simhah Bunem had been in the secular world, he had not been contaminated by it. For example, they admitted that R. Simhah Bunem had attended the theater and played cards. However, his disciples argued that he had done these things with his body but his mind had been concentrating on higher spiritual things.[31]

R. Simhah Bunem led the Przysucha School for thirteen years, from 1814 until his death in 1827. He implemented and developed the Yehudi's ideas, teaching an internalized intellectual form of spirituality which downplayed the external forms of Hasidism. The fundamental principle of one's spiritual development was the uprooting of arrogance and the desire for honor.[32] Public displays of piety and punctilious observance of the commandments were the epitomes of arrogance and the desire for honor. The Przysucha emphasis

28. See Assaf, "Ha-Hasidut be-Hitpathuta," 269–98.

29. In the first two generations of Hasidism, succession was from master to disciple. Gradually, this changed and succession became dynastic, from father to son. By the early part of the nineteenth century, the dynastic style became the dominant mode of succession. The dispute between Dov Baer of Lubavitch and Aaron of Starosselje was one of the earliest examples of this controversy. See Elior, "Ha-Mahloqet al Moreshet HaBaD," 166–86.

30. The most comprehensive study of R. Simhah Bunem's life and thought is Rosen, *The Quest for Authenticity.*

31. The stories concerning this period of Simhah Bunem's life are collected in Boim, *Rabbi Bunem mi-Przysucha,* I:23–82.

32. Brill, "Grandeur and Humility," 419–48.

on inwardness often manifested itself in rude, disrespectful behavior and the nonobservance of social amenities. Przysucha Hasidim mocked and derided those who in their eyes sought "honors."[33]

The desire to be free of arrogance sometimes led to the appearance of laxity in religious observance. This attitude is summarized in the following saying:

> What is the difference between the Hasidim of Kotsk and other Hasidim? The latter perform the commandments openly but commit transgressions in secret, while the Hasidim of Kotsk commit transgressions openly and perform the commandments secretly.[34]

The "transgressions" that the Przysucha and Kotsk Hasidim were accused of committing were in the realm of perceived laxity in not strictly adhering to the norms of religious observance of the other Hasidic groups. Two popular examples were, not strictly adhering to the time of prayer and speaking disrespectfully of other *zaddiqim*.

The Przysucha School's theology was as radical to its opponents as its social deviations. Kabbalistic tradition played a less significant role in the Przysucha curriculum. Its place was taken by the study of Talmud and the classics of medieval Jewish philosophy. *Maimonides' Guide for the Perplexed*, the *Kuzari*, and the writings of R. Judah Loewe (*Maharal*) of Prague were favorites. The writings of the latter had the greatest influence.[35] The ultimate goal of the Przysucha School was to mold an individual who would seek to know himself without illusions and find his own unique path to God. R. Simhah Bunem felt that "each Jew who sets out to worship God should dig a well in his own essence by means of which he will be able to cleave to his creator."[36]

R. Menahem Mendel of Kotsk summed up R. Simhah Bunem's style of leadership by observing that R. Simhah Bunem spiritually raised all who came to seek refuge in his shadow, but at the same time desired that each person raise himself up by himself.[37] The Przysucha School's emphasis on the Hasid's raising himself spiritually stands in sharp contrast to the

33. Rabinowicz, *Simhah Bunem*, 25–26.

34. Mahler, *Hasidism and the Jewish Enlightenment*, 292.

35. Rabinowicz, *Simhah Bunem*, 47. For Judah Loewe's influence on the Przysucha-Kotsk School, see Sherwin, *Mystical Theology and Social Dissent*, 51–55. On Maimonides' influence see, Dienstag, "Ha-More Nevuhim," 323.

36. Walden, *Toldot*, 14a.

37. E.E. No. 21.

prevailing Hasidic attitude that the *zaddiq* was the intermediary through whom the Hasid could attain a higher spiritual level.[38] In this respect, the Przysucha position was innovative in the history of Hasidism.

The Wedding in Ustilag

The seemingly uncivil behavior of the Przysucha Hasidim and their study of "dangerous" literature inflamed the indignation and fears of the *zaddiqim* who opposed the Przysucha path, and followed the path of popular *zaddiqism*. Their anger was so great that they wanted to excommunicate the Przysucha group from the main body of Hasidism. These opponents seized their opportunity at the wedding of the grandson of R. Abraham Joshua Heschel of Opatow, the senior *zaddiq* of the day, in Ustilag. Most of the *zaddiqim* and Hasidic notables in Poland and Galicia were in attendance at the wedding. R. Simhah Bunem was invited to defend his teachings and the practices of his followers. R. Menahem Mendel of Kotsk's forceful arguments dissuaded R. Simhah Bunem from attending. In his place, a delegation of five disciples, each distinguished in a different way, was sent: R. Isaac Meir of Gur, a Talmudic scholar; R. Feivel of Gryce, a scholar of Hasidism; R. Zusya of Schedlice, a wise man; R. Issachar Horowitz, who was wealthy; and R. Eleazar Baer of Grabowice, an eloquent speaker.

The main argument of R. Simhah Bunem's opponents was that the commandments of the Torah and the traditions of Hasidism were being denigrated in Przysucha. R. Isaac Meir and the other disciples argued eloquently that the Przysucha School was not guilty of the things they had been accused of by their opponents. R. Abraham Joshua Heschel, though swayed by their arguments, was not entirely convinced. He turned to R. Yerahmiel of Przysucha, the Yehudi's son, who had lost out to R. Simhah Bunem as successor to his father. He asked his opinion of R. Simhah Bunem and the charges against him. R. Yerahmiel spoke highly of R. Simhah Bunem, saying that he was filled with the spirit of the Torah and his actions were entirely for the sake of heaven. This testimony convinced R. Abraham Joshua Heschel, and he ruled in favor of Przysucha. This victory did not silence the criticism of the Przysucha School, but it did end attempts to question its fundamental legitimacy in the mainstream of Hasidism.[39]

38. For an analysis of this concept see, Rapoport-Albert, "God and the Zaddik," 296–325.

39. Rabinowicz, *Simhah Bunem*, 29–31. Also see, Berl, *R. Abraham Joshua Heschel*,

R. Menahem Mendel Succeeds R. Simhah Bunem

After R. Simhah Bunem's death in 1827, the question of succession again arose and split his disciples. Some chose R. Abraham Moses, R. Simhah Bunem's only son to be his successor, while the more intellectually inclined disciples looked elsewhere. R. Abraham Moses was a quiet, sickly, withdrawn personality. He died only fifteen months after assuming his position as *rebbe* and his place was taken by R. Isaac of Warka, the most important disciple of R. Simhah Bunem who had followed R. Abraham Moses. Though close personal friends, R. Menahem Mendel and R. Isaac had great differences in their approach to Hasidism. The following story illustrates their fundamental differences.

> R. Menahem Mendel followed the path of seclusion, while the path of his friend, R. Isaac of Warka, was that of associating with his Hasidim. They once met and R. Menahem Mendel said: my path is alluded to in the Torah; in the words *"they should take for me"* [Exodus 25:2]. If someone wants the path of truth, it is as Rashi comments, *"for me"* means, for my Name. The advice of *"terumah"* is to be separated from people, even the good ones.[40] Even from *"every man who would donate his heart"* [Exodus 25:2]. Isaac of Warka said: my path also is from this verse, *"they should take for me a donation [terumah]"* [Exodus 25:2]; from each one of them, to associate with them and to learn from them.[41]

Despite these differences and the mutual hostility of their followers, R. Isaac and R. Menahem Mendel continued the close friendship that had developed between them when they were disciple of R. Simhah Bunem, until the death of R. Isaac in 1848.[42]

R. Isaac Meir of Gur was also a distinguished disciple and there were those who thought that he was as worthy as R. Menahem Mendel to be R. Simhah Bunem's successor. The following story decribes how R. Isaac Meir decided to accept R. Menahem Mendel's leadership and convinced the other disciples to follow his lead.

46–50; Aescoli, *Ha*-Hasid*ut be-Polin*, 82–89. The most recent and comprehensive study of this episode is Gellman, "The Great Wedding," 567–94.

40. This is a play on the word *"terumah"* which means to contribute and to separate something as a holy offering.

41. See below, Sayings, 32, C.

42. See below, Sayings, 32, for more examples of the close relationship between them.

R. Hirsch Parczewer told: when the two great lights, R. Menahem Mendel and R. Isaac Meir of Gur once met, they sat for a
while. Then they went out for a walk in the woods. They remained
there alone for the whole night until dawn. When they entered
the house, R. Isaac Meir went in first and got the vessel for hand
washing and put a towel on his arm. He extended the vessel to
R. Menahem Mendel. At that point the assembly realized that
he was accepting R. Menahem Mendel as his master. After they
finished their meal, they locked themselves together in a room.
Outside, a loud argument was heard. Towards evening, the voice
of R. Menahem Mendel was heard. He said to R. Isaac Meir: In the
end, the leadership is between the two of us. Therefore, either I am
for you or you are for me. R. Isaac Meir responded: I am for you.
After a few minutes, R. Isaac Meir emerged into the room where
the whole assembly was waiting and told one of the Hasidim to
prepare to lead the afternoon prayers, since the *rebbe* will soon
come to pray. He said to the Hasidim: Don't be stubborn for nothing. Accept the leadership of the rabbi of Tomaszow and I will also
be under his leadership, since he is a true Jew.[43]

R. Isaac Meir remained R. Menahem Mendel's closest disciple until R.
Menahem Mendel's death. Only then did he become a *rebbe* in his own
right. The Gur Hasidic group became the most largest and most influential
Hasidic group in Poland from the end of the nineteenth century until the
destruction of Polish Jewry in the Holocaust.

R. Menahem Mendel in Tomaszow

After the leadership had been decided in favor of R. Menahem Mendel, he
returned to Tomaszow and attempted establish his court there. Tomaszow
had been his home for almost twenty years, since his marriage. R. Menahem Mendel continued the main themes that R. Simhah Bunem had established, though with a very different style. He had a fiery personality which
instilled awe and even fear in his followers. R. Simhah Bunem was kindly,
witty, and led his flock with good humor and love. In contrast, R. Menahem Mendel was angry, gruff, and led with fear. Yet there was a feeling
of tremendous spiritual energy in him that attracted many followers. As
a contemporary saying had it, "In Kotsk there burns a fire; a new light
is being established there."[44] One word was emblazoned on R. Menahem

43. See below, Sayings, 8, F.

44. Heschel, *Kotsk*, 2:450.

Mendel's banner—"Truth." He demanded that each person be true to God and to himself. His sharp personality attracted some people and repelled others. A disciple once explained R. Menaham Mendel's power in the following way: "Truth is like a nail, and the heart like an iron wall. In order to put the nail into the wall, one needs a very strong hammer. Our *rebbe* can drive a little truth in with the hammer."[45] The group in Tomaszow that followed R. Menahem Mendel was smaller than in Przysucha, but more spiritually intense and elitist. Most of the elitist sayings, like wanting only a handful of Hasidim who could attain great spiritual heights reflect the time in Tomaszow.[46] Several of R. Simhah Bunem's major disciples found R. Menahem Mendel's path too demanding. They said that it was like trying to comprehend a commentary on the Talmud without having first studied the Talmudic text on which the commentary is based. They eventually found their way to R. Isaac of Warka.[47]

Not everyone in Tomaszow was happy with R. Menahem Mendel's return to Tomaszow. Foremost among his opponents was the *zaddiq* R. Joseph of Yartszow, who also lived in Tomaszow. He was a longstanding critic of Przysucha and had been among the opponents of Przysucha in the deliberations during the wedding in Ustilag. Not only was he philosophically opposed to Przysucha Hasidism, but R. Menahem Mendel had the audacity to establish a court in his own backyard. The inhabitants of the city were also unhappy with the influx of Kotsker Hasidim. Unlike the custom in other Hasidic courts, the Hasidim did not just come for a Sabbath or festival visit, but would stay for long periods of time. In addition, they were poor and their presence did nothing for the economic well-being of the community, as was common in other towns that hosted Hasidic courts. Perhaps most disturbing of all was the behavior of Kotsker Hasidim, both social and religious. They were notorious for their lack of courtesy and strange behavior in public. Their religious behavior, not praying at regular times and other examples of seeming religious laxity also aroused the ire of the inhabitants of Tomaszow. Little more than a year after settling in Tomaszow, R. Menahem Mendel decided that the pressures were too great and he needed to find a new home, but where?[48]

45. Ibid., 2:520.
46. See below, Sayings, 11.
47. Gliksman, *Der Kotsker Rebbe*, 22.
48. Gliksman, *Der Kotsker Rebbe*, 22–24; Heschel, *Kotsk*, 2:445–51.

Kotsk

R. Menahem Mendel found his new home in Kotsk through the good offices of a disciple. R. Mattityahu Kuroner, who was rabbi in Kossov, became a widower. After a time, he married a rich widow who lived in Kotsk. Along with his marriage he became the rabbi of Kotsk. When he heard about Menahem Mendel's problems in Tomaszow, he proposed that he move to Kotsk. With a disciple as rabbi of the town, there would be no opposition to R. Menahem Mendel and his court. Another advantage of Kotsk was that it was not far from Warsaw and there was a good road to Kotsk. R. Menahem Mendel moved to Kotsk in 1829, and remained there for the rest of his life.[49]

Kotsk was not only a physical move, but also a psychological one. The spiritual radicalism of Tomaszow was tempered somewhat and Kotsk became more of a conventional Hasidic court. The numbers of visitors grew and R. Menahem Mendel's financial circumstances also improved.[50] This tempering of the radical impulse helps to explain the many stories about R. Menahem Mendel's activities that are more commonly associated with materialistic *zaddiqim*.[51]

During his first ten years in Kotsk, R. Menahem Mendel functioned more or less like other *zaddiqim*. He accepted petitions, gave advice and comforted his followers, in addition to teaching daily classes in Talmud and commentaries. However, not all was well with him. Periods of depression and melancholy grew in intensity and frequency. R. Menahem Mendel felt the burden of leadership more intensely and the demands of leading such a large group sapped him spiritually. R. Menachem Mendel described his spiritual state through the following parable.

> There was once a Jew who had a snuffbox made of goat horn. He lost the snuffbox and went around bemoaning his loss. "Woe is me. Not only do we live in the darkness of exile, but such a fate had to befall me, to lose my wonderful snuffbox." The holy goat came to him. This goat wanders the earth and has horns which reach the heavens and kiss the stars. The goat, seeing the Jew crying, bent down and said to him, "Cut off a piece of my horn and make yourself a new snuffbox."
>
> The Jew cut off a piece of horn, made a new box, and put his snuff into it. Consoled, he went to the *bet midrash* and offered the

49. Gliksman, *Der Kotsker Rebbe*, 24–25.

50. Heschel, *Kotsk*, 2:451.

51. See below, Sayings, 63.

worshippers some snuff. Jews took some snuff and were full of awe. Such snuff! A taste of paradise! Such a thing has never existed! And the box is beautiful. Where did you get the snuffbox?

The Jew told the story of the snuffbox and the holy goat. The whole crowd dashed out of the *bet midrash* in search of the holy goat. The goat, as was its custom, wandered around the world with its long horns touching the skies and kissing the sun, the moon, and the stars. The crowd caught it and bound it with ropes. The holy goat was good-natured and let everyone take a piece of horn. Everyone took a piece and made a snuffbox. Among the Jews there was joy and gladness. But the holy goat wanders the world without horns.[52]

R. Menachem Mendel saw himself as the goat of the parable. His followers may have gained something positive from their journey to Kotsk, but the psychic cost was too great for him. His response to this spiritual draining was to seclude himself periodically until he finally did so almost permanently in the fall of 1839.[53]

There is no debate about the basic fact that R. Menahem Mendel spent the last twenty years of his life more or less in seclusion, rarely venturing from his private study in the synagogue in Kotsk. However, there are two radically different descriptions of the event that led to his seclusion. The first is a historical event, supported by the sources, while the second is a myth that came to be known as the "Friday Night Incident."

R. Mordecai Joseph Leiner of Izbica and Simhat Torah

Central to the historical account is R. Menahem Mendel's relationship with one of his closest disciples, R. Mordecai Joseph Leiner. R. Mordecai Joseph was born in Tomaszow, in 1800. He developed a close friendship with R. Menahem Mendel, who was like an older brother. It was R. Menahem Mendel who introduced R. Mordecai Joseph to Hasidism and took him to the court of R. Simhah Bunem. Mordecai Joseph was counted among the senior disciples in Kotsk and was treated with great respect by all. R. Isaac Meir of Gur, R. Menahem Mendel's most intimate disciple/colleague asked R. Mordecai Joseph to serve as a go-between in a delicate situation. R. Isaac Meir wanted to suggest his wife's sister as a bride for the recently widowed

52. Heschel, *Kotsk*, 2:535; Fox, *R. Menahem Mendel mi-Kotsk*, 43–44. Both attribute it to oral traditions.

53. Heschel discusses the issue of depression at length. See *Kotsk*, 2:523–55.

R. Menachem Mendel.[54] R. Mordecai Joseph's efforts were successful and R. Menahem Mendel married R. Isaac Meir's sister-in-law. The union was blessed with four children.

When the group of disciples in Kotsk grew too large, R. Menahem Mendel sent the younger ones to R. Mordecai Joseph for spiritual direction. He also taught a daily class in Talmud.[55] When R. Menahem Mendel was in seclusion, Hasidim often turned to R. Mordecai Joseph for advice and help. At a Friday night gathering in the fall of 1838, R. Menahem Mendel collapsed. He spent the next nine months in bed. During R. Menahem Mendel's illness, R. Mordecai Joseph began to accept petitions (*kvitlech*) and donations (*pidyonot*) from Hasidim, who were now coming to him in greater numbers for advice and help.[56] R. Mordecai Joseph's actions created ambivalence in the other senior disciples which subsequently turned to open anger and opposition. They believed that R. Mordecai Joseph was preparing to rebel against R. Menahem Mendel and become a *rebbe* in his own right.[57] Yet, the other disciples did not publicly censure R. Mordecai Joseph. Many years later, R. Samuel of Sochaczew asked his father, R. Abraham of Sochaczew, R. Menahem Mendel's son-in-law and one of the senior disciples in Kotsk, why the other disciples had not rebuked R. Mordecai Joseph. R. Abraham answered that the disciples had remained silent because they feared that their motives might not be totally pure ("for the sake of heaven"), but might be influenced by jealousy or personal hostility.[58]

If R. Menahem Mendel was aware of R. Mordecai Joseph's dissatisfaction, he said nothing in public. Others, however, began to see the impending rift. R. Hanokh Henokh of Aleksandrow later reported that he once met R. Mordecai Joseph coming out of R. Menahem Mendel's study as he was on his way in. R. Hanokh Henokh asked R. Mordecai Joseph if there was anything new. He continued: "When he answered me that there was nothing new, I knew at that moment that he was no longer a disciple of Kotsk."[59]

54. Alter, *Meir Eynei ha-Golah*, I:69–70 (paragraph 225).

55. Levin, *Ha-Admorim mi-Izbica*, 18. This is how many of the people who left with R. Mordecai Joseph when he split with R. Menahem Mendel first became attached to him.

56. Accepting petitions and donations is to declare that one considers himself to be a *rebbe*.

57. Gliksman, *Der Kotker Rebbe*, 53; Levin, *Ha-Admorim mi-Izbica*, 32.

58. *Shem mi-Shmuel, Mezora*, 5:196.

59. Levin, *Ha-Admorim mi-Izbica*, 30.

For a disciple to visit his master and leave without learning anything was a sure sign that the disciple was not "listening" to his master.

In the fall of 1839, R. Mordecai Joseph came to spend the High Holy Days in Kotsk as he had done in previous years. Exactly what happened during this holiday season is a subject of controversy. All the sources are in agreement that after *Simhat Torah* R. Mordecai Joseph left Kotsk, having irreparably broken with R. Menahem Mendel, founding his own dynasty in the aftermath. There are two very different and contradictory accounts of this crucial period. The first version is the Leiner family tradition found in *Dor Yesharim*. According to this account:

> When the time came for his greatness to be revealed, in the year 5600 of the creation, to which the *Zohar* had alluded [that the gates of wisdom will then be opened],[60] he traveled to Kotsk. It was his custom to be in Kotsk from *Rosh Hashanah* until the end of *Succoth*. This last time, many Hasidim immediately began to address him with the title *rebbe* and to give him petitions with donations. When he accepted the petitions, a great tumult and much disputation broke out among the Hasidim, for jealousy resides even in the heavens. God-fearing and wise Hasidim followed him and cleaved to him. He behaved in this manner [as a *rebbe*] in Kotsk until *Shemini Azeret*, and the *rebbe* [R. Menahem Mendel] said nothing.
>
> On the eve of *Simhat Torah*, R. Mordecai Joseph told his followers to bring Torah scrolls to his inn, where they would pray and conduct the *haqafot*, instead of joining the others in the *rebbe's bet midrash*. They did not understand the reason for this at the time, but carried out his wishes immediately. After the prayers in the *rebbe's bet midrash* the *haqafot* began. R. Mordecai Joseph usually led the *haqafah* of Joseph the Zaddiq.[61] When the time came for this *haqafah*, R. Menahem Mendel ran from his room into the *bet midrash* and grabbed the Torah scroll from the person who was holding it. When he saw who was holding it, he immediately returned it, saying that he thought it was R. Mordecai Joseph. The Hasidim saw this and understood that R. Mordecai Joseph had foreseen this with divine inspiration, and therefore had made his own *minyan* in his inn, in order to avoid a dispute. R. Mordecai Joseph said that had he been holding the Torah scroll, there is no

---

60. *Zohar*, I:119a.

61. In the Hasidic and kabbalistic tradition, the seven *haqafot* (circuits with the Torah scroll) were dedicated to the seven "shepherds" (Abraham, Isaac, Jacob, Moses, Aaron, Joseph, and David). The sixth *haqafah* dedicated to Joseph also symbolized the *zaddiq* (the *sefirah* of Yesod). See, Yaari, *Toldot Hag Simhat Torah*, 290, 317–318.

way it could have been taken from him. Later, he told his Hasidim that he had received a sign from heaven that he should not go to the *haqafot* in the *rebbe's bet midrash*. When he was preparing to go to the *haqafot* in the *bet midrash* he put on his left shoe first, before his right shoe.[62] From this he understood that he should not go, but should celebrate the *haqafot* in his own house.[63]

J. L. Levin agrees with the general tenor of this account, but has a different version of the dramatic confrontation between R. Mordecai Joseph and R. Menahem Mendel. Levin asserted that he was reporting an eyewitness account, but he did not cite his source. According to Levin's version, R. Mordecai Joseph did participate in the *haqafot* in R. Menahem Mendel's *bet midrash* and was prepared to lead the sixth *haqafah*, that of Joseph the *Zaddiq*. He had just put on his *talit* when R. Menahem Mendel came over and pulled the *talit* off his shoulders.[64] R. Mordecai Joseph took the *talit* back, put it on, and left for his inn, where he and his followers completed the *haqafot*.[65] Regardless of which version is the correct one, R. Mordecai Joseph left Kotsk immediately after *Simhat Torah*, never to return. R. Menahem Mendel retreated to his study and secluded himself there for the rest of his life. Whatever inner turmoil had been troubling him, the confrontation with R. Mordecai Joseph Leiner, his old friend and disciple, was the straw that broke the camel's back and drove R. Menahem Mendel into seclusion. R. Mordecai Joseph Leiner was the only major disciple to leave Kotsk. R. Menahem Mendel's other disciples remained loyal to him until his death. Major figures like R. Isaac Meir of Gur, R. Abraham of Sochaszow, R. Hankokh Henokh of Aleksander and other figures who went on to found the major Hasidic dynasties in Poland, did not officially become "*rebbes*" until after the death of R. Menahem Mendel.

---

62. The *Shulhan Arukh* (*Orah Hayyim* 2:4) prescribes how one should dress. The right shoe is always put on before the left. R. Mordecai Joseph was normally punctilious in following these rules.

63. Leiner, *Dor Yesharim*, 33–34.

64. During the *haqafot*, only the person leading the *haqafah* wears a *talit*. R. Menahem Mendel pulled the talit off R. Mordecai Joseph to indicate that he did not want R. Mordecai Joseph to have the honor of leading the *haqafah*. R. Menahem Mendel's action was a public humiliation and repudiation of R. Mordecai Joseph.

65. Levin, *Ha-Admorim mi-Izbica*, 31.

The Friday Night Incident

A completely different story of what lead to R. Menahem Mendel's seclusion is the so-called "Friday night incident." According to this story, on a Friday night in the fall of 1839, R. Menahem Mendel either desecrated the Sabbath by extinguishing the candles or knocking over the kiddush cup on a Friday night, and made a statement denying God. I have demonstrated in a study of the history of this legend that it has no historical basis and is a complete fiction. My study also traces how this legend was disseminated and popularized.[66] It was first widely disseminated by R. J. L. Slotnick in 1918. It was then picked up by Martin Buber and uncritically repeated by other authors in following years. Joseph Opatoshu's novel, *In Polish Woods*, which was one of the great Yiddish literary successes of the interwar period, is situated in the 1820s–1840s, and R. Menahem Mendel and his court in Kotsk are a major subtext of this novel. This novel was also an important source for the dissemination of the "Friday Night Incident." Elie Wiesel in his *Souls on Fire* continued the tradition of the "Friday Night Incident" and his treatment of this issue is typical. He does not explicitly say that R. Menahem Mendel did something antinomian. Rather, he hints and winks saying that "something happened."[67] By now, this story has been repeated so many times that it is believed and repeated by virtually all authors writing about R. Menahem Mendel, even though there is *not a shred of evidence* to support it. Heresy and discontent within the upper echelons of the Hasidic world were not an alien phenomenon in the history of Hasidism.[68] However, no reliable evidence has been submitted to suggest that this was the case in Kotsk. On the other hand, there is no reason to doubt the basic facts of the confrontation between R. Menahem Mendel and R. Mordecai Joseph on *Simhat Torah* of 1839, once the hagiographic elements are removed.

The *Kvitel*

A document that has recently received renewed attention recently sheds new light on the relationship of R. Mordecai Joseph and R. Menahem Mendel and what led to his departure. This document, a *kvitel* that was given by an older Hasid to R. Abraham Mordecai, the son of R. Yehudah

66. My extended study of the history of the "Friday Night Incident" is found in the Appendix.

67. Wiesel, *Souls on Fire*, 228–31.

68. See Assaf, *Ne'ehaz be-Svakh*.

Aryeh Leib, the author of *Sefat Emet*, when he assumed the leadership of the Gur School of Hasidism. This Hasid, Ya'akov Yizhak of Vallahovek, presented this spiritual autobiography on the occasion of his first meeting with the new rebbe in Gur in 1905. He described his spiritual journey from his first encounter with R. Menahem Mendel of Kotsk as a seventeen year old until the time of this meeting. What is important for the present discussion is one passage in which he describes a central teaching of R. Menahem Mendel that he heard from Kotsker Hasidim whom he considered reliable transmitters of Kotsker traditions.[69]

What is most striking about this short teaching is that it could serve as a summary of the core teachings of R. Mordecai Joseph's theology.[70] It demonstrates that the conflict between R. Menahem Mendel and R. Mordecai Joseph was not about theology, but was more about personal issues.[71] Temperamentally, they were very different people. R. Mordecai Joseph was very mild-mannered and non-confrontational in contrast to R. Menahem Mendel who was famous for his impatience and direct manner. These differing temperaments could easily have led to tensions over leadership style and how one should treat disciples. We know that R. Menahem Mendel was not the warmest person and his personality could be overwhelming. We also know that R. Menahem Mendel was subject to periods of depression and withdrawal. Perhaps R. Mordecai Joseph reached a point where he could no longer accept R. Menahem Mendel's style of leadership. When R. Isaac of Warka asked R. Mordecai Joseph why he had left Kotsk, he responded that he had been commanded by Heaven to lead a community of Hasidim.[72] Though there is some ambiguity in this response, the emphasis is on leadership, not on teachings or theology.

The anger and sense of betrayal on the Kotsker side would also tend toward a personal explanation. It is a commonplace of human psychology that the smaller the real differences between two competing groups, the greater the sense of anger and hostility. When one of the Kotsker disciples came back to Kotsk after having left with R. Mordecai Joseph, R. Menahem Mendel said to him, "'Reverence for your teacher is like reverence for Heaven [*Avot* 4:12].' Are there two Heavens?[73]" The hostility between the

69. The text of this passage is found below in the section on Kotsker Theology.

70. Faierstein, *All is in the Hands of Heaven*, chapter 4.

71. Faierstein, "Kotsk–Izbica Dispute," 75–79.

72. S.S.K. 1:63, 4:84.

73 S.S.K. 4:68–69; E.E. No. 119.

followers of Kotsk and Izbica continued for many years and were reconciled only at the turn of the twentieth century.[74]

In summary, the available evidence appears to indicate that the dispute between R. Menahem Mendel and R. Mordecai Joseph was an issue of style and personality rather than theological differences. Both of them continued the theological traditions of the Przysucha School.

The Period of Seclusion

Even during the last twenty years of his life following the incident with R. Mordecai Joseph, R. Menahem Mendel's seclusion was not total. He still performed many of his functions as a *rebbe*, though in a much diminished and erratic manner. Hasidim would still be greeted, but might have to wait weeks before R. Menahem Mendel appeared in public, and then only briefly. Occasionally, he would storm into the *bet midrash* and scream at the Hasidim who happened to be there, demanding to know why they were there and what they wanted of him.[75]

R. Menahem Mendel's relationship to his family and close disciples was more normal, even during the long periods of seclusion. He celebrated the Passover *seder* with his family, and on the Sabbath he would examine his grandchildren on their studies of the previous week. His senior disciples were able to enter his room and often consulted him on a variety of matters. He corresponded with a number of people and kept himself informed on developments in the wider world.[76]

R. Menahem Mendel died on 22 *Shevat* 1859. He was succeeded by his son, R. David, as *Rebbe* of Kotsk. David did not follow his father's path, but reverted to material *zaddiqism*. R. Menahem Mendel's spiritual legacy was continued in a somewhat attenuated manner by the dynasties of his disciples, Gur, Sochaszow, Alexander and others.[77] Ironically, it was R. Mordecai Joseph Leiner, R. Menahem Mendel's disciple who left him who most closely continued to teach the more radical ideas of R. Menahem Mendel.[78]

---

74. See, Faierstein, *All Is in the Hands of Heaven*, 2005, 24–26.

75. Heschel describes Kotsk during this period. See, *Kotsk*, 2:547–51.

76. Gliksman, *Der Kotsker Rebbe*, 63–67 provides examples and documentation.

77. See Piekarsz, "Inner Point," 617–60, for an analysis of this development.

78. Faierstein, *All Is in the Hands of Heaven*, 1989/2005.

R. Menahem Mendel's Teachings

Hasidic Literature

Hasidic literature is composed of two primary genres, teachings and stories. The teachings are normally in the form of sermonic commentaries on verses in the weekly Torah portion. They were delivered in Yiddish at various gatherings and later translated into Hebrew for publication. *Zaddiqim* rarely wrote or published their own teachings. In the majority of cases the teachings were copied and collected by disciples who published them, often after the death of the *zaddiq*. The largest group of Hasidic texts are in this genre. These works are also known as the theoretical literature of Hasidism and are the primary source of its religious teachings.

The other major genre of Hasidic writings are the collections of hagiographic stories about the *zaddiqim*. They rarely have theological teachings interspersed with the stories. This body of literature was created by a diverse group of authors, some by Hasidim and others by writers had no connection to Hasidism but wrote whatever would sell in the marketplace. These collections of stories began to be published in the 1860s and became popular as an accessible form of entertainment and edification. The typical hagiographical collection consists of stories about one individual arranged in a loose chronological order or a collection of stories about a group of individuals who are somehow connected. It might be the members of a dynasty or a major figure and his disciples whose stories are collected.[79]

The historical reliability and veracity of this hagiographical literature is questionable. Typically there is a lack of source documentation or evidence that the author had any direct connection to the hero of the book. More problematic is that one can find the same stories retold about several different figures. The same wonder stories and miraculous qualities are attributed to many different figures, as if the author was working from a template. Jewish neo-romantics at the beginning of the twentieth century, like Martin Buber and M. J. Berdichevsky, "discovered" these Hasidic story collections and mined them as a source to create a form of Judaism that was more amenable to their conceptions, reinventing Hasidism in their own image. Martin Buber was the most influential figure in this movement and the best known advocate for the hagiographic literature as a legitimate source for the history of Hasidism. Gershom Scholem and other scholars

---

79. Nigal, *The Hasidic Tale.*

have argued that this literature is not a historically reliable source.[80] There are even differences of opinion among modern scholars about the extent to which the Hasidic hagiographical literature can be relied upon as a historical source. Two important scholars of Hasidism, Moshe Rosman and Immanuel Etkes, both wrote biographical studies of Israel Baal Shem Tov, the founder of Hasidism. An important point of difference between them was their approach to the hagiographical literature and its reliability as a historical source. Rosman takes a more skeptical approach, while Etkes is more willing to accept the assertions of hagiographical works like *Shivhei ha-Besht*.[81] Each author signals his perspective through his title.[82] This debate continues and a resolution is beyond our concerns, but an awareness of this central issue in the writings of diverse authors on Hasidism is important in understanding the sometimes conflicting conclusions that are encountered in the literature.

Kotsker Teachings and Stories

Attempting to understand and analyze the teachings of R. Menahem Mendel of Kotsk presents many of the problems of other Hasidic literature. There are also other concerns. The first and most important problem is that he left no writings. In this, he followed the example of his teachers, the Yehudi and R. Simhah Bunem of Przysucha, who also left no writings. According to a great grandson, R. Menahem Mendel did not like writing down his teachings. Another great grandson put it more poetically. He said that R. Menahem Mendel wanted to inscribe his teachings on the hearts of his disciples and not on paper. His son, R. David, and other family members also followed this tradition of not writing down their teachings.[83] There is a legend that R. Menahem Mendel wrote down his teachings all year and then burned them on the eve of Passover with the *hametz*. Heschel cites this story without giving a source. Most likely, he heard it as an oral legend.[84] Interestingly, there is a documented story of R. Isaac Meir of Gur doing

80. For some critiques of Buber's approach to Hasidism see, Scholem, "Martin Buber's Interpretation of Hasidism," 227–50; Katz, "Martin Buber's Misuse of Hasidic Sources," 52–93. For Buber's response to his critics, see, "Replies to My Critics," 731–41

81. *Shivhei Ha-Besht* [In Praise of the Baal Shem Tov], first published in 1815, is the hagiographical biography of the founder of Hasidism.

82. See, Rosman, *Founder of Hasidism*; Etkes, *The Besht*.

83. Gliksman, *Der Kotsker Rebbe*, 35–36.

84. Cf. Heschel, *Kotsk*, 2:490.

exactly the same thing. He burned a volume of his writings on the eve of Passover together with the *hametz*.[85] This is a good example of a problem common in Hasidic hagiography, one story is attributed to more than one figure. In this case, the evidence that R. Isaac Meir did this act is reliable, but there is no evidence that R. Menahem Mendel did such a thing.

Another issue is that many of his immediate disciples who wrote books, notably R. Isaac Meir of Gur and R. Abraham of Sochaszow, did not mention R. Menahem Mendel or his teachings. The teachings and stories about R. Menahem Mendel that have been preserved were scattered like small nuggets in a wide diversity of writings. Several enterprising authors collected these diverse teachings and stories in volumes devoted to R. Menahem Mendel and other important figures of Przysucha—Kotsk Hasidism. Each succeeding collection cast its net wider and included more stories.

The Problem of Authenticity

The late Jacob Levinger devoted two important articles to the problem of the authenticity of what has been written about R. Menahem Mendel and his teachings.[86] Levinger observed that there are five significant collections of Kotsker material. The earliest, *Ramatayim Zofim*, was published in 1881. Its author, R. Samuel of Shinove, was a secondary disciple of R. Menahem Mendel. He relates approximately thirty sayings and stories. The next collection, *Ohel Torah*, collected approximately 300 hundred sayings and stories from a variety of other sources. It is also the only collection that indicates the source that it is citing. *Emet ve-Emunah*, contains approximately 900 teachings and stories. *Amud ha-Emet*, has approximately one thousand items. *Emet mi-Kotsk Tizmah*, has over twelve hundred items. One other significant source of Kotsker material not mentioned by Levinger is *Siah Sarfei Kodesh*. It is a collection of teachings and stories relating to the whole Przysucha-Kotsk School and the many figures associated with it, and is a significant source for Kotsker material.

In response to this mushrooming growth of sayings, Levinger examined some of these purported Kotsker sayings and showed that many of them were sayings and stories that were also attributed to a variety of other Hasidic figures. In response to this problem, Levinger suggested a number of criteria to cull out of this mass of material, the teachings and stories that

---

85. Alter, *Meir Eynei ha-Golah*, I:82 (paragraph 258).
86. Levinger, "Authentic Sayings," 109–35 and "Teachings," 413–31.

can be attributed to R. Menahem Mendel with a fair degree of certainty. His criteria are based on the relationship of the author to R. Menahem Mendel. A good example would be R. Samuel of Sochaczow, author of *Shem mi-Shmuel*, the son of R. Abraham of Sochaczow, R. Menahem Mendel's son-in-law, and one of his closest disciples. Thus, he can be considered a reliable source for the teachings of R. Menahem Mendel. Levinger concludes that there are approximately seventy-five authentic teachings in the *Shem mi-Shmuel* and another ninety in the writings of a number of other authors that he considers authentic transmitters of Kotsker traditions.[87] Thus, Levinger considers approximately 15 percent of the material that has been transmitted in the name of R. Menahem Mendel is authentic.

An additional concern for Levinger is that when one analyzes the teachings that meet his criteria for authenticity, very few of them display the theological radicalism that one associates with "Kotsk." This is particularly evident in the material from the *Shem mi-Shmuel*, the work that would seem to have the best pedigree, being written by R. Menahem Mendel's own grandson. This is not surprising as it might seem at first blush when one considers the subsequent history of Polish Hasidism. There was a retreat from the theological radicalism of Kotsk among R. Menahem Mendel's disciples. As R. Isaac Meir of Gur put it, "the Kotsker led with awe and fear, I lead with Torah."[88] Elements of Kotsker teachings remained, but the fervor was tamed. R. Isaac Meir of Gur and R. Samuel of Sochaszow were both prolific authors who wrote important works of halakhic responsa and Talmudic novellae, but did not write any Hasidic teachings. It was only the next generation of Sochaszow and Gur leaders that returned to writings Torah commentaries in the traditional Hasidic form, exemplified by the *Shem mi-Shmuel* and *Sefat Emet*.

Levinger's reservations must be taken seriously, but one is still left with the problem of determining if the sayings and stories attributed to R. Menahem Mendel accurately reflect his teachings and personality. The most comprehensive study of Kotsker teachings is the late Abraham Joshua Heschel's Yiddish two-volume study, *Kotsk: The Struggle for Integrity*. Heschel addressed this problem in the introduction. His solution was to rely on his intuition, which was based on his experience. Heschel writes that in his youth he still had the opportunity to interact with old Hasidim who had been to Kotsk and passed on to him an understanding of Kotsk as a

---

87. Levinger quotes the texts in the appendices of his two articles.

88. See below, Saying, 35, B.

living experience. I have relied on Heschel's opinions in that I have utilized those collections that Heschel considered reliable and cited regularly in his work. Nonetheless, one must approach this material with a certain amount of agnosticism. There is the constant problem of sorting out sayings that are attributed to multiple figures. *Siah Sarfei Kodesh*, is a veritable gold mine of multiple attributions. Sometimes one can find the same story or saying attributed to several people in the space of a few pages. I have not attempted to check all the stories for multiple attributions. In any event, there would be no way of determining the priority of attributions. Just because it is attributed to an earlier figure would not necessarily argue for the earlier figure's priority. The bottom line is that I believe that one can speak with a fair degree of confidence that these teachings reflect the spirit and attitudes of the Przysucha-Kotsk School of Hasidism. However, as with much of Hasidic literature, there is no ultimate certainty that specific teachings attributed to a particular figure actually originated with that person.

The Selection of Texts

The teachings attributed to R. Menahem Mendel and the stories about him range from one-line comments to several paragraphs long. There are approximately a thousand separate items in the texts from which I have chosen to draw stories and teachings.[89] Not all of the texts are appropriate for translation in a volume aimed at the non-specialist reader. There are many teachings that are comments or reflections on Talmudic or other rabbinic texts that are not easily explainable or relevant to the non-specialist in Rabbinic literature. There are also a number of sayings that are based on a play on words, whether in Hebrew or Yiddish, that are untranslatable without extended explanations or commentary. The majority of these sayings do not shed any light on R. Menahem Mendel's teachings, but are scholarly bon mots or witty puns on Biblical or rabbinic passages. The selection criterion utilized was whether a particular text or story would be comprehensible to the non-specialist reader and no effort has been made to shape the narrative in a specific direction. I have included both theological teachings and stories, endeavoring to be inclusive. I have added explanatory comments to some texts and stories, which give historical background or explain specific terms or concepts. My comments are within brackets [ ] under the teaching

---

89. A list of texts can be found in the Bibliography (A. Primary Sources).

or story that I am commenting on and in a smaller font to distinguish my comments from the original texts.

Kotsker Theology

It is extremely difficult if not impossible to construct a coherent comprehensive theology from the fragmentary sayings and occasional stories about R. Menhem Mendel. He was not a systematic thinker and made no effort to construct a theoretical basis for his ideas. Similarly, there are many stories about the religious practices of Kotsker Hasidim. Many of these stories were disseminated by opponents of Kotsk and intended to mock them or put them in a negative light. It is not always easy to decide if stories about the more extreme practices were true or merely negative propaganda. Despite these difficulties, certain patterns and themes emerge from the teachings and stories. Among the themes that are important in Przysucha-Kotsk Hasidism are God, Worship, Torah Study, what is Hasidism and what does it mean to be a Hasid, along with other themes that one would expect to find in the teachings of any Hasidic group. The emphasis might vary, but all of these themes would be found. However, the theme that exemplifies Przysucha-Kotsk Hasidism and gives it its unique character is the concept of individualism.

R. Menahem Mendel explained how one worked toward this spiritual goal. His method for finding one's own "spiritual truth" was described in a *kvitel* given to the *rebbe* of Gur by an old Hasid who had spent time in Kotsk in his youth. This Hasid writes:

> I have heard from true Hasidim, who heard the following statement from the holy master of Kotsk, of blessed memory, which was uttered early, at the time when his sun began to shine in Tomaszow. This is what he said [in Yiddish]: "The heart must be broken; both shoulders must be crushed and heaven and earth totter and yet one must not depart from one's own." Thus far his holy words. The Hasidim who heard this from the holy master did not know what he meant by this. He replied as follows: "It is stated in the writings of the holy Rabbi Isaac Luria, that the majority of souls have been created only to put right one or two character traits which they had corrupted in this world in this world and if they fail in this they will be obligated to undergo a further transmigration in this world." He said further: "How can a man know which character trait he has been created to put right and elevate in this world? It is that which his inclination entices him constantly to transgress."

He said in Yiddish, as follows: "That which causes him trouble to carry out provides him with clear evidence that it is this for which he was created to put right and to elevate and for this self-sacrifice is required."[90]

The concept that one is obligated to repair a specific commandment that one has violated in a previous transmigration is central in the teachings of R. Isaac Luria and his kabbalistic School. Luria was famous for having the ability to gaze at someone's forehead and know their whole spiritual history and more importantly, what sin they have been brought into the world to repair.[91] However, he was unique in this ability and even his closest disciples were unable to accomplish this. Finding his own sin and repairing it was a major concern for R. Hayyim Vital, Luria's closest disciple. He devotes significant space in his spiritual diary, the *Book of Visions*, to the sin that he had to repair and how he endeavored to accomplish this.[92]

In Lurianic kabbalah, the process of individual spiritual repair and redemption is known as *tikkun*.[93] In the beginnings of Hasidism, this concept is a significant theme in the teachings of the Baal Shem Tov and his immediate disciples, notably R. Jacob Joseph of Pollnoye. The term *geulah pratit*, personal redemption, is used there for this process of personal spiritual growth.[94] In later generations of Hasidism, this process was seen as an elitist task that was only appropriate for *zaddiqim*. The ordinary person would attain their redemption by cleaving to the *zaddiq* (*devekut*), who will bring his disciples with him on his spiritual ascent. Perhaps the most important divergence of the Przysucha-Kotsk School from the Hasidic mainstream was its rejection of the concept of the *zaddiq* as spiritual middleman. The *zaddiq's* task in Przysucha-Kotsk was to be a spiritual guide and mentor, enabling each Hasid to seek his own *tikkun*. Each Hasid has a sin to repair that is unique to himself. Thus the spiritual quest must also be individualistic. There is a tradition that R. Simhah Bunem would tell the story of R. Yekel of Cracow to every young man who came to Przysucha.[95] This is a

---

90. Jacobs, *Heads in Heaven*, 106–7.

91. Fine, "Metoposcopy," 79–101.

92. Faierstein, *Jewish Mystical Autobiographies*, 156–64.

93. Fine, "Tikkun," 4:35–53. The contemporary usage of this term, as in "*Tikkun Olam*" is not related to the kabbalistic concept. Fine discusses this issue at length in his article.

94. Faierstein, "Personal Redemption," 214–24.

95. Berger, *Simhat Israel*, 49.

famous folktale that predates R. Simhah Bunem. The essence of the story is that R. Yekel had a dream that there was a great treasure under a bridge in Prague. After several adventures, he meets a guard at the bridge who tells him that he also had a dream about a treasure under the stove in the house of a Jew in Cracow. R. Yekel realizes that he is talking about his house and returns home. He looks under the stove and discovers the treasure. The moral for R. Simhah Bunem was that one must look within for the treasure. One does not need to travel great distances or seek great teachers to find truth. It is within us, if we know how to look.

Kotsker Religious Practice

The following five practices formed the practical expression of Kotsker Hasidism. They were the core of the path that the Hasid followed in order to attain his own spiritual goals:

1. The fundamental principle was the study of Torah. The study of Bible, Talmud, and its commentaries.[96] All Kotsker Hasidim would study day and night, or more precisely, night and day, since the primary time of study was at night, when other people slept, so that nobody would see them studying.

2. Intention and thought. Everyone must be do things with sense, with thought, with reflection and profundity. Discarding the external and striving for the essence, for inwardness, to know what is primary and what is secondary, throwing away the shell, the husk, to separate the wheat from the chaff.

3. To minimize the recitation of excessive prayers, *tehinnot*, *piyyutim* and *yozerot*.

4. One must be critical. One must test everything that one does. One should not imitate anyone thoughtlessly, out of habit. One should not follow everything that is accepted out of a foolish piety, like an ignorant pietist.

5. To distance oneself from the ignorant masses. Kotsker Hasidim did not want to be acceptable to other people, even though others had

96. One of the unusual features of Przysucha-Kotsker Hasidism is that they did not study the *Zohar* or other kabbalistic texts. It was considered appropriate only for a very small elite who had attained the highest spiritual levels. See, Jacobs, *Heads in Heaven*, 106.

little respect for them. On the contrary, they presented themselves in such a way that others should think that they were changing Jewish customs, in order that others should speak ill of them and separate themselves from them. This was their desire, to remain isolated among themselves in their own group and have no relations with others.[97]

Anything that distracted the seeker was to be discarded or relegated to the background. Family obligations, social convention, even respect for parents and teachers could be sacrificed if they became a distraction or impediment in the quest. As R. Menahem Mendel taught, it was not meant for everyone, but only for those whose desire to seek the Truth was so strong that they were ready to make any sacrifice that might be necessary.

A Modern Approach to Kotsker Teachings

To the modern reader, R. Menahem Mendel may be reminiscent of a Zen master who teaches by his personal example and pushes his disciples to greater wisdom through short sayings that demand study and reflection, like Zen *koans*. The place of meditation in Zen is taken by Talmud study in Kotsk. Perhaps one approach to understanding Kotsk and its teaching is to treat the individual teachings like Zen *koans*. Each teaching must be considered on its own merits. After a certain amount of reflection one sees a message in the teaching or not. If there is no resonance, one puts the teaching aside. Perhaps it might resonate later. If not, there is nothing wrong with this. Not every teaching was meant for every person. As we have seen, a core Kotsker teaching was that each person has one or two spiritual issues that they must address and perfect. R. Menahem Mendel taught that one learns what one's issues are from what arouses strong emotions when confronted with that commandment or experience.

That having been said, one must never forget that R. Menahem Mendel was a Hasidic *zaddiq*, who functioned like other *zaddiqim*. The editors of the collections had no problems with including stories about R. Menahem Mendel that portray him as a wonder working *zaddiq*, no different from the "materialistic *zaddiqim*" that Przysucha-Kotsk Hasidism supposedly opposed and from which it differentiated itself. Perhaps this seeming paradox is more a reflection of modern desires and expectations rather than the nineteenth-century reality. R. Menahem Mendel may have

97. Graubart, "Hizdiku et ha-*Zaddiq*," 7–8. Quoted in Gliksman, *Der Kotsker Rebbe*, 34.

expressed ideas and concepts that resonate with contemporary people, but we must never forget that he and his disciples were pious nineteenth-century East European Jews, with all that it implies.

II. The Teachings Attributed to
R. Menahem Mendel of Kotsk

1. Arrogance

A.

The evil inclination of arrogance is found primarily among people who have already transcended other inclinations. [L.T. 425 n. 12; E.E. No. 43]

[The Hebrew term *"yezer"* (inclination) is applied here to a wide variety of desires and inclinations, such as wealth, power, and material wants.]

B.

It is difficult to understand why Balaam did not convert after he foretold the greatness of Israel at the end of days? [Num 23:7–10, 21–24] The answer is as the Talmudic sages say in *m. Avot* [5:19], *"the disciples of the evil Balaam are arrogant."* He did not convert because of his arrogance. The word *ger* [convert] is derived from the word for dragging or towing, that is, it is secondary. Balaam wanted to be the most important and the head and not to be dragged after Israel. [S.S.K. II:88; E.E. No. 202]

[Balaam was the gentile prophet who was hired to curse Israel by Balak, king of Moab, and instead wound up blessing them against his will (Num 22:2—24:25).]

C.

In the verse, *"you shall be wholehearted [tamim] with the Lord your God"* [Deut 18:13], the letter *Tav* is larger than normal. He said in a humorous way. This is so that the whole world should be able to enter the *Tav*, except for the arrogant person, because he is even greater. [S.S.K. III:24; E.E. No. 154]

[*Tav* is the first letter of the word "*Tamim*" and in the Torah scroll this letter is larger than normal.]

D.

We find in the prayer book: "He brings down the arrogant to the earth and raises up the humble to the Heavens." That is, the arrogant, even if they are brought down to the earth, they remain arrogant and that is why they are brought down endlessly. Not so the person who is essentially humble. Even if he is raised up, nonetheless he remains in his humble state. As Scripture says, "*I am unworthy of all the kindness*" [Gen 32:11]. That is why the humble are raised to the Heavens. [R.Z., *Elijah Zuta*, II, ch. 14, 40; O.T. 16]

2. Asceticism

[Asceticism was not a virtue in itself. Rather, in Kotsk it was a by-product of an indifference to the world outside of Torah study. Anything that took one away from this ideal was to be disparaged and dismissed.]

A.

R. Menahem Mendel once said: I can take a young man immersed in the pleasures of the world and make them so disgusting to him, that he will not even be able to hear about these things. If he would hear about it, he would vomit up his food. [E.E. No. 666]

B.

R. Menahem Mendel almost never went to sleep or changed his clothes. He would fall asleep during study or worship. He would wear the same coat for years. [E.E. No. 692]

C.

It is easier for the body to endure all kinds of asceticism and deprivation than it is to endure the yoke of the kingdom of Heaven. [L.T. 427 n. 38; E.E. No. 245]

D.

Following the path of Torah is the greatest form of asceticism for the body. [E.E. No. 51]

3. Business

[The first passage seeks to explain the paradox of the next two passages. In his personal life, R. Menahem Mendel failed in the business endeavors he undertook before he became a *zaddiq*. In contrast, his mentor, R. Simhah Bunem of Przysucha, was very successful in business and traveled to Danzig and other fairs to engage in business. The last passage is the ideal to be desired by the Hasid for whom earning a living is a necessity.]

A.

He was once asked how he knew to give advice to Hasidim who came to him for business advice and questions about mundane matters. Since he was completely separated from the mundane world, how did he know about these matters? He answered that one who is outside the mundane world can look into it, since one who is outside of something can see into it. However, one who is inside cannot see the matter. [S.S.K. I:70; E.E. No. 734]

B.

Hirsch Leib Kotsker once came from Warsaw and R. Menahem Mendel asked him about what news he had heard and also about the prices of wheat and other crops. When he left, R. Menahem Mendel said to Hirsch Tomaszower: "Hirsch Leib was here and said that Nicholas has died." Hirsch immediately ran after Hirsch Leib and asked him about this. Hirsch Leib said that he knew nothing about this and he only told R. Menahem Mendel about crop prices. Several hours later, a messenger came to Kotsk with the news that the Czar Nicholas had died. [E.E. No. 49]

C.

One year the astrologers predicted that in a short time the world would end. For this reason, businessmen ceased doing business and the markets fell badly. A big businessman from Germany came to the *Rebbe* of Kotsk and asked his advice, if he should disregard this rumor or not. The *Rebbe* responded that he should not pay attention to the opinions that the world would end. Indeed, the man listened to him and became very wealthy. [S.S.K. IV:57; E.E. No. 112]

D.

If a person follows the just path, he does not think about or burden his thoughts with business, he only finds a way to sustain himself. [S.S.K. II:87; E.E. No. 200]

4. Darkness

A.

"*Darkness is not dark for You*" [Ps 139:12]. When we understand that the darkness is from ourselves, then we can transform the darkness into light and it will not be dark. [E.E. No. 817]

[Darkness is another way of speaking about depression. It challenged Menahem Mendel all his life. The last twenty years of his life when he was in seclusion was the result of depression.]

B.

"*He set bounds for darkness*" [Job 28:3]. God left a corner in the darkness where we can sustain ourselves. [S.S.K. I:74; E.E. No. 766]

5. Death

A.

Death is nothing. It is like going from one room to another and choosing to go to the nicer room. [S.S.K. II:94; E.E. No. 205]

[This attitude is consistent with the Kotsker indifference to the physical world.]

B.

R. Menahem Mendel asked someone who wanted to immigrate to the land of Israel, what was the reason that motivated him? He responded that Jacob wanted to be buried in the land of Israel because he wanted to avoid rolling through the earth in expiation of his sins. R. Menahem Mendel asked him in a surprised tone of voice: you love your body so much that that you are concerned with the suffering of the body even after death? [N.H. 51; S.S.K. IV:110; E.E. No. 126]

C.

If King David had put the Book of Psalms in the proper order, one could have resurrected the dead through the recitation of the whole Book of Psalms. [E.E. No. 230]

6. Delaying Time of Prayer

[Delay in the proper time of prayer was a characteristic of the Przysucha-Kotsk School of Hasidism from its beginnings. It was known for not praying at the appointed times, but waiting until they felt spiritually prepared. It was a source of conflict and tension with non-Hasidim and also with other Hasidic groups. The three answers given here reflect three different audiences and situations.]

A.

R. Leibele Eger asked R. Menahem Mendel what reason he could give his grandfather, R. Akiva Eger, for delaying the time of prayer. The reason for his grandfather would have to be based on *halakhah* and not on Hasidic thought. Tell your grandfather that we find in Maimonides' [*Mishne Torah*] concerning a workman who works for a boss and sharpens his blade all day that the sharpening is also required for the work. [E.E. No. 135]

[R. Akiva Eger, rabbi of Posen, was one of the most important Talmudic scholars in the first half of the nineteenth century and a strong opponent of Hasidism. His grandson became a Hasid, much to the chagrin of his family. As R. Menahem Mendel said, a halakhic scholar deserves a halakhic answer and offered one to R. Leibele Eger.]

B.

After Joseph, the brother of R. Isaac Meir of Gur, died, he came to his family in a dream and told them that he has no rest from the Rabbi of Apta over the delay in the time of prayers. R. Isaac Meir said that when he came a second time, he should be told that the answer is that he traveled to Kotsk; this was the custom there; he followed it, and the *Rebbe* of Kotsk has broad shoulders. [E.E. No. 109]

[The second response is very much in the Hasidic mold. It is the responsibility of the *zaddiq* to defend his followers, especially when they follow his traditions. R. Menahem Mendel said that if R. Meir of Apta, who was known as one of the strongest opponents of the Przysucha-Kotsk School, had any complaints he should direct them directly to R. Menahem Mendel.]

C.

To the author of the book, *Kav Hen*, he gave the following answer. He begins the prayers at the appropriate times, but what can he do if he is not able to finish until after the appropriate time. [E.E. No. 136]

[The third response is the most surprising one. Its almost apologetic tone is uncharacteristic of Kotsk. The *Kav Hen* is a book of Hasidic teachings by R. Noah of Karov.]

D.

In tractate *b. Berakhot* [14b]: "Ulla said, whoever reads the *Shema* without phylacteries, it is as if he testified falsely about himself. Said Rabbi Hiyya bar Abba in the name of Rabbi Johanan, it is as if he had offered a burnt offering without its meal offering or a sacrifice without its libations." R. Menahem Mendel was asked: If so, what about the Hasidim who read the *Shema* in the morning without phylacteries? They are testifying falsely. He responded that there is an apparent difficulty in the language of the Talmud. "Said Rabbi Hiyya bar Abba" and not Rabbi Hiyya bar Abba said, as is customary in the Talmud. However, the explanation is that Rabbi Hiyya bar Abba did not come to argue with Ulla, but to explain his words. When he said, "it is as if he testified falsely" only if he offered the burnt offering without any meal offering at all. However, this teaches us that if he had brought the meal offering, even after a period of time, he still fulfilled his obligation. This is also the rule with the *Shema*. That is, only if he never donned that whole day. However, if he dons phylacteries later in the day, he has fulfilled his obligation. [E.E. No. 201]

[This is a learned way of justifying the apparently unusual behavior of Kotsker Hasidim regarding prayer and its appropriate times and rituals that called forth criticism from other Hasidic groups.]

7. Demons

A.

R. Menahem Mendel once explained a passage in Maimonides' writings. He wrote that there are no demons, but there are many discussions of demons in the Talmud. R. Menahem Mendel explained that indeed there once were demons, but after Maimonides ruled that there are no demons, they agreed with him in Heaven. Therefore, they no longer exist. [E.E. No. 670]

[This is an ingenious method of harmonizing two contradictory statements by two important authorities whose teachings were considered beyond questioning. Whether it was meant to be taken seriously or not, it is creative. It is also in accord with the Hasidic notion that "the *zaddiq* decrees and God fulfills."]

8. Discipleship

A.

R. Menahem Mendel used to say about himself that he was a *talmid hakham* [scholar], because he was a *talmid* [disciple] of R. Simhah Bunem of Przysucha who was a *hakham* [wise]. [S.S.K. IV:57; E.E. No. 110]

B.

The *Rebbe* of Aleksandrow told that he once had a dream that he was in Tomaszow. R. Menahem Mendel was sitting in his chair and R. Simhah Bunem of Przysucha was standing behind his chair. He ran to him, with tears, and called out, give me a *Rebbe*. He pointed with his finger to R. Menahem Mendel. He awoke and immediately traveled to Tomaszow. When he entered, R. Menahem Mendel said to him: now you know who the *Rebbe* is after Przysucha. He immediately accepted him as his *Rebbe*. [E.E. No. 279]

C.

R. Isaac Meir of Gur said: I saw a pillar of true fire and I accepted its authority. When I came to Tomaszow, I saw several hundred youths engaged in the study of Hasidism. It was clear to me that each one of them could have been as great as the Baal Shem Tov, but apparently the opposition of people injured them [spiritually]. [E.E. No. 796]

D.

A certain *zaddiq* asked R. Isaac Meir of Gur why he still needed to be a disciple of R. Menahem Mendel, since he was worthy to be a *zaddiq* on his own. He responded, it is written, *"purchase truth and do not sell it"* [Prov 23:23]. Purchase as long as you can purchase. Only when it is no longer found to be purchased, then you can sell. Therefore, as long as I can purchase, I am not yet ready to sell. [E.E. No. 738]

E.

A certain person asked R. Isaac Meir of Gur if he still needed to be a disciple of R. Menahem Mendel. He responded: *"the designs in a man's mind are deep waters."* This is the Rabbi of Kotsk. *"But a man of understanding can draw them out"* [Prov 20:5]. [E.E. No. 776]

F.

R. Hirsch Parczewer told: when the two great lights, R. Menahem Mendel and R. Isaac Meir of Gur once met, they sat for a while. Then they went out for a walk in the woods. They remained there alone for the whole night until dawn. When they entered the house, R. Isaac Meir went in first and got the vessel for hand washing and put a towel on his arm. He extended the vessel to R. Menahem Mendel. At that point the assembly realized that he was accepting R. Menahem Mendel as his master. After they finished their meal, they locked themselves together in a room. Outside, a loud argument was heard. Towards evening, the voice of R. Menahem Mendel was heard. He said to R. Isaac Meir. In the end, the leadership is between the two of us.

Therefore, either I am for you or you are for me. R. Isaac Meir responded: I am for you. After a few minutes, R. Isaac Meir emerged into the room where the whole assembly was waiting and told one of the Hasidim to prepare to lead the afternoon prayers, since the *Rebbe* will soon come to pray. He said to the Hasidim: Don't be stubborn for nothing. Accept the leadership of the Rabbi of Tomaszow and I will also be under his leadership, since he is a true Jew. [E.E. No. 791]

[R. Isaac Meir was a close contemporary of R. Menahem Mendel's and his closest disciple. When R. Simhah Bunem died, there were those who put forward R. Isaac Meir as his potential successor. This story describes how R. Isaac Meir decided to be R. Menahem Mendel's disciple rather than a *Rebbe* on his own. By publicly showing that he was ready to serve R. Menahem Mendel was a way of acknowledging R. Menahem Mendel as his master. R. Isaac Meir only became a *Rebbe* in his own right after the death of R. Menahem Mendel. The Gur School went on to become the most influential School of Hasidism in Poland.]

9. Divine Providence

A.

R. Menahem Mendel said: if a person sticks a staff into a pile of sand and then pulls out the staff and does not believe that every grain of sand falls back into a place chosen for it by Heaven, one must suspect that he might be a heretic. [E.E. No. 801]

10. Egotism

A.

Mishnah Yoma, chapter 2, *mishnah* 1, says: "Originally, whoever wanted to clear the ashes from the altar did so. If two were equal, the officer said to them, raise the finger, etc. It once happened that two were equal and they ran up the ramp and one of them pushed his colleague and he fell, breaking his leg, etc." It would appear that in the later generations there was greater self-sacrifice to serve, so that they even courted danger. Perhaps it is the opposite. He responded that in truth the earlier generations were greater. They did not have such egotism that they should do the service, only that the service be accomplished and the will of God fulfilled, whether by himself or by his colleague. However, in the later generations, each one wanted that he should do the service and not someone else. [S.S.K. II:91–92; E.E. No. 203]

11. Elitism

[Though Hasidism has been portrayed as a populist movement ever since the rise of Romantic neo-Hasidism at the end of the nineteenth century, most widely expressed in the influential writings of Martin Buber, it always contained within itself an elitist component. The elitist element is most openly expressed in the Hasidism of Przysucha-Kotsk. At the same time, as is seen in other statements there was also a place for ordinary people in Kotsk. These statements are more hopes and dreams rather than expressions of reality.]

A.

He once said to R. Wolf of Strykow about himself that he thought that he would have fifty or one-hundred-and-fifty disciples who would stand on the roofs and attain the level of the prophets. [S.S.K. I:27; E.E. No. 679]

B.

Toward the end of his life, R. Menahem Mendel said. I thought that I would have four hundred disciples. I would go with them into the forest; feed them manna, and they would recognize the power of God's kingdom. [S.S.K. III:15; E.E. No. 145]

C.

He said: I have Hasidim who can point to heaven and say: "*This is my God and I will enshrine Him*" [Exod 15:2]. [S.S.K. I:97; E.E. No. 216]

D.

There was once a very large group of Hasidim surrounding R. Menahem Mendel's door, all wanting to greet him. Suddenly, he opened the door and called for his son-in-law, the Rabbi of Sochaczew to come in to his room. He pointed at the crowd and said: in my younger years, they would not have been able to approach me. Now, what has become of me? See that you should develop yourself to a higher spiritual level. [E.E. No. 167]

E.

In the beginning, the Hasidim of Tomaszow were all worthy to be on the level of the greatest *zaddiqim*. However, the [evil] eye of the world hurt them. [S.S.K. I:81]

F.

The Rabbi of Sochaczew told that his father-in-law, R. Menahem Mendel, once said: I thought that I would have three hundred disciples like the Baal Shem Tov and if not that, at least like Moses of Litomirsk, who was then sitting in front of him. [E.E. No. 329]

G.

R. Menahem Mendel once opened the door to his study suddenly and screamed at those in the *bet midrash*. I imagined that I would only have a minyan of disciples dressed in white, and no more. They all ran away from great fright. The only one who remained was the Rabbi of Gostynin who was not able to run away. R. Menahem Mendel said to him: I wasn't talking about you. [E.E. No. 664]

12. Envy

A.

R. Menahem Mendel said: A person is born with envy. Lusts come from becoming accustomed and growing up with them. [L.T. 427 n. 40; E.E. No. 249]

13. Enthusiasm

A.

The Talmudic sages said:[1] The Holy One took the image of a fiery coin from under the Heavenly Throne and showed it to Moses. He said: this is what they should give, like this. The issue is that Moses was surprised that a half shekel should be an exchange for the soul; that is everything that

1. Midrash *Tanh.*, *Ki Tisa* 9.

a person should give for his soul. Therefore, the Holy One showed him a coin made of fire. That is, He explained that the giving should be with enthusiasm. [E.E. No. 409]

14. Evil/Evildoers

A.

He said to someone. "*Shun evil and do good*" [Ps 34:15]. First you have to be someone who shuns evil and then you have to be someone who hates evil. When you reach the level of "*do good*," then we will help you. [S.S.K. III:19; E.E. No. 227; 868]

B.

"*Am I only a God near at hand, says the Lord, and not a God far away*" [Jer 23:23]? "*Near at hand*"—this is the righteous one. "*Far away*"—this is the evildoer. The intention is that if I want the righteous one who is close to me, then I also want the evildoer who is far from me. [L.H. 73; E.E. No. 541]

15. Evil Inclination [*Yezer Hara*]

A.

One day R. Menahem Mendel came to the *bet midrash* and saw a Hasid studying. He asked him what he was studying. The Hasid responded that he was studying the verse, "*if the thief is seized while tunneling*" [Exod 22:1]. Menahem Mendel said: The meaning seems to me that if a person digs, he will find the thief, who is the evil inclination. [S.S.K. I:67; E.E. No. 714]

B.

"*He took what was at hand as a present for Esau*" [Gen 32:14]. Whoever takes what come to hand, without reflecting on whether the matter is good or not, even if he think it is a *mitzvah*, this is not good. Rather, it is an offering to Esau that strengthens the evil inclination. [S.S.K. III:25; E.E. 161]

42

C.

In *parshat Behaʾalotekha* it is written: "*When you are at war in your land, etc. . . . you shall sound the trumpets, . . . and be delivered from your enemies*" [Num 10:9]. In *parshat Taizi*, it is written: "*When you take the field against your enemies and the Lord your God delivers them in your power and you take some of them captive*" [Deut 21:10]. This verse does not mention any human actions. The difference is that when the person begins to war with the evil inclination, he is certain that he will be victorious and take it captive. He may even be worthy to bring it into holiness and transform it to good, as the verse says, "*with your whole heart*" [Deut 6:5]. However, if the person waits until the inclination comes to him and only then begins to war with it, then he will not vanquish it easily. Only if, "*you shall sound the trumpets,*" and call out to the Lord and pour out your heart and soul before the Holy One, then you will be saved. [E.E. No. 71]

D.

R. Menahem Mendel once said. I once thought that I would have such Hasidim that when the evil inclination would come to them, they would not listen to it. Not because they would not want to listen to its advice but because they would not have time for it, like R. Hirsch Baer Grawitzer. [E.E. No. 852]

16. Exile

A.

Each person needs to exert himself in the study of the chapters concerning the exile and redemption from Egypt because it was the preparation for all the exiles of the community of Israel. One can learn from all of its details how to get through the exile. [E.E. No. 291]

17. Faith

A.

He interpreted the verse in Psalms, "*Abide in the land and remain faithful*" [Ps 7:3]. Lie in the earth and feed yourself with faith. [S.S.K. I:69; E.E. No. 726]

[The original Yiddish phrase for "lie in the earth" is "*lig in drerd.*" It has no direct English translation. It has the meaning, to find oneself in trouble or distress. He means to say, no matter how bad the condition you find yourself in, sustain yourself with faith in God.]

B.

"*Who can find a faithful man?*" [Prov 20:6]. A man of faith who is truly faithful can't be found because he is truly hidden. [E.E. No. 318]

[The truly faithful person is also humble and does not stand out. Therefore, he can't be found.]

C.

He once said about the contemporary *zaddiqim*. They say that they see the seven shepherds, the *Ushpizin*, in the *sukkah*. I have faith. Faith is clearer than seeing. [S.S.K. I:66; E.E. No. 715]

[Seeing the Biblical figures that represent the seven lower *sefirot* (*Ushpizin*) who are symbolically invited into the *sukkah* each night of the festival is a sign of the mystical attainment of the *zaddiq*. This is in accord with the general tendency of Kotsker Hasidism to denigrate supernatural claims by *zaddiqim* and those made on their behalf by their Hasidim.]

D.

"*When Pharaoh let the people go, etc . . . the people may have a change of heart when they see war and return to Egypt. So God led the people roundabout, by way of the wilderness . . .*" [Exod 13:17–18]. The "*war*" can be interpreted to mean the war with the Evil Inclination. The Israelites were not yet completely rooted in their faith and that is why He feared that they might return to Egypt. Therefore, "*So God led the people roundabout, by way of the wilderness*" that they should receive the Torah and study with Moses so that they would become completely rooted in their faith. [O.T. 32; E.E. No. 359]

E.

At the end of tractate *Menahot* it says: "it is all one whether a man offers much or little, as long as he directs his mind to Heaven" [*m. Menah.* 13.11]. Even if he offers much, he must still direct his mind to Heaven. [E.E. No. 398]

18. Fear of Heaven [*Yirat Shamayim*]

A.

He once asked a Hasid if he had ever seen a wolf. The Hasid responded, yes. R. Menahem Mendel asked him if he feared the wolf and he responded, yes. He asked the Hasid further, if he remembered that he was afraid and the Hasid responded that he remembered nothing because of the fear. Menahem Mendel said to him that his fear of heaven should be such that he would not feel the fear when he fears the Lord. [S.S.K. I:66; E.E. No. 712]

B.

Once a Hasid came to Kotsk who had been very rich, had lost his fortune, and was now in dire poverty. Several important Hasidim entreated R. Menahem Mendel that the *Rebbe* should pray for him. R. Menahem Mendel responded: If he is a Hasid and God fearing, then he lacks nothing. [S.S.K. I:70; E.E. No. 731]

C.

"All is in the Hands of Heaven except for the fear of Heaven" [*b. Ber.* 33b]. That is, when a person asks for children, health, or livelihood, it is in the hands of Heaven whether or not the Lord wants to respond to his request. However, if a person asks God with his whole heart and soul that he should receive fear of Heaven into his heart, he can be certain that his prayer will not be in vain and he will receive fear of Heaven immediately. [S.S.K. I:75; E.E. No. 491]

D.

If a person has fear and is afraid of anything in the world aside from the Lord, His Torah, and the commandments that he has commanded us, he is in the category of an idol worshipper. The Torah says: "*The Israelites caught sight of the Egyptians advancing up on them, greatly frightened the Israelites called out to the Lord*" [Exod 14:10]. The Israelites called out because they saw that they had a fear other than of the Lord. [S.S.K. I:76]

E.

The fraternal meals of the Hasidim are similar to the fasts of the *mitnagedim*. The essence of the fast is for the group to search and examine the deeds of the group to see if they are appropriate and repent of their bad deeds. Since this was a regular activity, the Hasidim established something similar through their communal meals. Their association is in order to bring the fear of Heaven into the hearts of their colleagues and for them to repair their ways. [S.S.K. I:81]

[*Mitnagedim* [lit. opponents] was the name given to the opponents of Hasidism. One of the centers of this ideology was in the Lithuanian yeshivas. In contrast to Hasidic optimism, their outlook was essentially pessimistic. Thus, Hasidim feasted while the *mitnagedim* fasted with the same spiritual reasons.]

F.

R. Isaac Meir of Gur said: The Talmudic sages said [*b. Rosh Hash.* 17a]: "it is forbidden to inflict excessive fear on the community that is not for the sake of Heaven." If you will ask, R, Menahem Mendel inflicted fear! However, it was completely for the sake of Heaven. [E.E. No. 277]

G.

"One who earns his living from his labor is greater than one who fears Heaven" [*b. Ber.* 8a]. He asked: why is the shoemaker who sits at his bench greater, since he does not occupy himself with Torah? He answered that the reason is that the one who earns his living from his labor is greater, because here, in this world he only does things with hands composed of matter. However, his mind ascends to Heaven and he is a man of God. This is greater than the one who is God fearing without work. [S.S.K. III:26; E.E. No. 163].

H.

"*How abundant is the good that you have hidden away for those who fear you*" [Ps 31:20]. R. Menahem Mendel said: that you have hidden away the fear [of heaven]. If it were not so, there would be no reward and punishment, since everyone would be God fearing and there would be no free choice at all. [N.H. 154; E.E. No. 550]

I.

"*If you return, etc. and do not waver*" [Jer 4:1]. R. Menahem Mendel said: If you will turn away from material things, you will fear God and you will not be able to waver. [L.H. 72]

J.

"*If you search for it as for treasure, then you will understand the fear of the Lord*" [Prov 2:4–5]. R. Menahem Mendel said: If someone has a treasure and it is buried deep, he exerts himself to find the treasure because he is certain that there is a treasure. He should exert himself in the same way to find the treasure of fear of Heaven, since he will certainly find it. [L.H. 77]

K.

"*The fear of the Lord is pure, abiding forever*" [Ps 19:10]. R. Menahem Mendel said: If it abides forever, then we know that it was pure. If not, it will not last. [S.S.K. III:26; E.E. No. 165].

L.

R. Menahem Mendel once asked R. Isaac of Warka (or vice versa), what did King Solomon innovate in the Book of Proverbs? There are enough ethics to be found in the Torah. He responded that the primary innovation of the Book of Proverbs is to teach us that nobody is smart in comparison to God. Concerning King Solomon it is written, "*he was the wisest of men*" [1 Kgs 5:11], and "*in his old age, his wives turned his heart*" [1 Kgs 11:4]. This teaches us a great lesson. A person who is very wise should be very careful that he does not turn, heaven forbid, from the path of God, as a result of his great wisdom. [E.E. No. 718]

M.

"*Your clothes should be white at all times and do not lack oil on your head*" [Eccl 9:8]. You should always think that you are wearing costly white silk garments and a jar full of oil is placed on your head. If you will divert your attention for a moment and not be careful, the oil will spill over your clothes and ruin them. The fear of God should be the same. It is forbidden to divert your attention, for in a moment you can ruin yourself. [E.E. No. 828]

N.

Feivel the *shamash* once pleaded on behalf of a wealthy Hasid who had lost his wealth, that R. Menahem Mendel should bless him. He responded: if I would say so, it would happen. When Feivel heard this he said: so decree it and it will be fulfilled. R. Menahem Mendel responded in a loud voice: how can I go against the will of Heaven? [E.E. No. 837]

[This statement is particularly difficult to understand. Is R. Menahem Mendel saying he has no power to influence Heaven? There are many examples of him demonstrating his powers in this regard. (See below Sect. No. 63. "The Zaddiq and His Powers.") A Hasid might say that this was his way of deflecting his disciple. He saw that this was the will of Heaven and he felt that he could not or should not interfere.]

19. Free Will

A.

"I once entered a ruin and Elijah came and watched at the entrance until I had finished my prayers" [*b. Ber.* 3a]. The question is, why did he not come to him before he entered the ruin and tell him not to enter? It would seem that the heavenly practice regarding the person is that they send him to this world and he is allowed to do what his heart desires, free will is given. Only afterwards, when he leaves this world do they ask him, what have you done? [E.E. No. 578]

20. God

A.

A Kotsker Hasid would shout, "Father, Father" during his prayers. A second Hasid said about him jokingly: perhaps He is not his Father, since when we don't do the will of God we are called servants and not children. R. Menahem Mendel heard this and responded: we shout Father so many times until He becomes our Father. [S.S.K. IV:29; E.E. No. 85]

B.

He said: "*You shall have no foreign God*" [Ps 81:10]. God should not be a stranger to you. [R.Z., *Elijah Zuta*, II, ch. 14, 39, n. 10; E.E. No. 20]

C.

R. Menahem Mendel once asked the great rabbis of his generation, where does God live? They laughed at him. "*His presence fills all the earth*" [Isa 6:3]. He responded: the Holy One lives where he is allowed in. [S.S.K. I:71]

D.

R. Menahem Mendel once asked: where does God live? He responded to his own question: the Holy One lives where he is allowed in. Then he continued: "*let Him not find anything unseemly among you and turn away from you*" [Deut 23:15]. Just like a human king, if barrels of refuse stand before the person's door, how can the king enter his house? [E.E. No. 641]

E.

The Talmudic sages said, "Every place you find God's strength, you also find his modesty" [*b. Meg.* 31a]. R. Menahem Mendel asked, it is written, "*The Lord king is grandeur*" [Ps 93:1]. Where do you find modesty here? However, it is written He is robed in grandeur. That is, the grandeur is only a garment, but His inner essence is modesty. [S.S.K. IV:21; E.E. No. 82]

F.

He once said about the Talmudic passage: "On whom should we rely, only on our Father in Heaven" [*b. Sotah* 49a]. He said: whoever knows this, lacks nothing. [S.S.K. I:86]

G.

To someone who offered excuses concerning some matter, he said: it is possible to offer excuses to a mere mortal, but how will he be able to offer excuses before God who examines the heart and knows one's thoughts. [S.S.K. II:23; E.E. No. 178]

H.

R. Menahem Mendel once said: the difference between a Hasid and a *mitnaged* is that the Hasid fears the Holy One, while the *mitnaged* fears the *Shulhan Arukh*. [S.S.K. V:44; E.E. No. 645]

I.

One morning R. Menahem Mendel said: "*Mode ani lefanekha*" [I am thankful before you].[2] He then said, who am "I" and who is "before you" and he paused and spoke no further. [S.S.K. V:45; E.E. No. 647]

[The essence of a person's worship is to see his own humbleness and the greatness of God.]

J.

"*The Lord made me lord of all Egypt*" [Gen 45:9]. We need to understand why Jacob did not know himself that Joseph was the lord of Egypt. I heard in the name of R. Menahem Mendel of Kotsk, that Joseph said: I made the Holy One the Lord of all Egypt so that all the Egyptians would recognize that the Holy One is in the whole world. [N.H. 49]

2. A prayer recited upon awakening in the morning.

K.

"*The earth is full of Your creations*" [Ps 104:24]. The person can acquire You in the whole world. Your glory is recognizable in everything since You alone created everything, and only You. There is the recognition in everything that without your energy, there is no life or existence in the thing. [E.E. No. 562]

L.

"Whoever does not have land, is exempt from the Festival pilgrimage to the Temple [*Re'iyah*]" [*b. Pesah.* 8b]. This is because if he is not connected to the land, he does not need to make the pilgrimage. This is in every place where he is connected to the Holy One and is not connected to physicality. [E.E. No. 588].

M.

"*Keep in mind that the Lord alone is God in Heaven*" [Deut 4:39]. The meaning is that a person should recognize in his soul that the Lord is God. [S.S.K. III:25; E.E. No. 160]

N.

"*Listen to me and I will give you counsel*" [Exod 18:19]. The most important advice is to listen to My voice. [E.E. No. 214]

O.

"*Know therefore this day, etc., . . . there is no other*" [Deut 4:39]. The meaning is that in all of the reality of the world there is no reality other than the reality of God. Everything that a person sees with his physical eyes is not reality at all. Only what he sees with his intellectual eyes is reality. [E.E. No. 486]

P.

"His secret is fairness; His advice is faith; His work is truth."[3] This means that God's fairness is hidden. Since we don't understand the fairness, which

3. This passage is from a prayer for the High Holy Days.

according to our understanding is the opposite, His advice is faith. The advice is the faith to believe that His work is truth. [E.E. No. 517]

Q.

"And Jacob sent the angels before him" [Gen 32:4], that they should leave him since he did not need their help. The Holy One can help without angels and without cause. [E.E. No. 314]

R.

"You listen to the desires of the humble, O Lord, and prepare their hearts" [Ps 10:17]. God prepares the heart of whoever desires God. [E.E. No. 545]

S.

It is written, *"Come to Pharaoh"* [Exod 10:1]. Why is it not written, go to Pharaoh. This is because with regard to God, going is not relevant, since *"His Glory fills the Earth"* [Isa 6:3]. [E.E. No. 234]

21. God and Israel

A.

"Please forgive the offense of the servants of the God of your father" [Gen 50:17]. Why is the servant of God not mentioned in the Torah until this point? When Jacob wanted to reveal the end of history, his children said, *"Hear O Israel, the Lord our God, the Lord is one"* [Deut 6:4]. It was then that the tribes accepted the yoke of the Kingdom of Heaven upon themselves. [*b. Pesah.* 56a] That is why Scripture began to call them servants of God. [E.E. No. 351]

B.

"Then Moses sang" [Exod 15:1]. The Midrash says: The angels wanted to sing songs of praise to God. The Holy One said to them. Moses and the children of Israel will sing first and then the angels. [*Exod. Rab.* 23.7] The reason is that the angels are ready at all times, but Israel, only when the desire is awakened. If they are delayed, then the desire will pass. [E.E. No. 369]

C.

"All your deeds should be for the sake of Heaven" [*m. Avot* 2.12]. The "for the sake of Heaven" should also be for the sake of Heaven. [E.E. No. 602]

D.

R. Menahem Mendel asked the Rabbi of Radzymin. R. Jacob, for what reason was the person created in the world? He responded: the person created in the world in order to repair his soul. R. Menahem Mendel said in a loud voice: R. Jacob, is this what we learned from our master in Przysucha? The person created in the world in order to praise Heaven. [E.E. No. 739]

E.

"*I pleaded with the Lord at that time saying, O Lord God, etc.*" [Deut 3:23–24]. That he is able to say God is Lord to the last moment. [E.E. No. 774]

22. Government

A.

During the wedding of his son Moses, of blessed memory, they waited a long time until R. Menahem Mendel went out from his room to the wedding ceremony. When he got there, he asked those present, what is the meaning of "pray for the welfare of the government, for were it not fear of it, etc." [*m. Avot* 3.4]? When nobody answered him, he said: the meaning is, only when there is peace for the government do we need to pray that they should not issue bad decrees, since when they are engaged in wars, they are preoccupied. [E.E. No. 260; 616]

[This reflects the situation of the Jewish community living under the domination of the Czarist government and its attempts to "reform" the Jewish community in the first half of the nineteenth century.]

B.

R. Abraham of Ciechanow told that R. Isaac Meir of Gur and the Rabbi of Ciechanow decided that the decree regarding clothes was like apostasy and it was necessary to martyr oneself for it, if necessary. He traveled to Kotsk and R. Menahem Mendel asked him what they were thinking about this new decree? What does your rabbi say about this and how did he rule halakhically? He responded that the rabbi traveled to Warsaw to discuss this matter with R. Isaac Meir. He asked, what did they decide? R. Abraham was afraid to answer. R. Menahem Mendel screamed at him, why don't you answer? He said that they decided that one needed to martyr oneself. R. Menahem Mendel grabbed the end of his beard and shouted loudly, is this how they ruled? They studied the subject and saw this rule? I also once looked into a book and I also have some idea in abstruse matters and I didn't see any law there that one should be martyred for this. How could two such great scholars waste the blood of Israel? It would be more appropriate that they should squeeze the community of Israel a bit and the redemption will come. [E.E. No. 270]

[This incident relates to the Russian "Clothing Law" of 1846. It was not specifically addressed to Jews, but affected the whole populace of the Russian Empire, and was part of a larger modernization effort. It tried to modernize the mode of dress of the populace and two basic styles of dress were authorized for men, the "German" and the "Russian merchant." Ultimately, the Jews adopted the "Russian merchant" style mandated by the government. The other option, the "German" required one to be clean-shaven and wear a short jacket, while the "Russian" version included a long coat, boots, a tall fur hat and allowed a beard. This is also why Hasidic groups outside the Russian Empire, in the Austro-Hungarian Empire that had no "clothing laws," retained a more archaic style of dress, including white knee britches, a different style of *shtreimel* and other clothing differences.]

23. Hasidim

A.

The Rabbi of Kotsk was asked. Why was there such great love among the Hasidim in the past and is not found so much in our day? He responded that there is a Palace of Love in Heaven and the holy Rabbi of Berdichev opened this palace. This was the cause of the great love among the Hasidim. However, when the evildoers began to utilize this love in order to do contemptible things, the *zaddiqim* of the generation gathered and closed this Palace. [L.T. 424 n. 6; S.S.K. I:26; E.E. No. 36]

B.

The first time R. Yehiel Meir of Gostynin came to visit R. Menahem Mendel, he was very concerned that it would be very difficult for him to accept the behavior and practices of Kotsker Hasidim. R. Menahem Mendel said to him: We do not innovate anything. We only illuminate what someone comprehends. [S.S.K. I:66; E.E. No. 711]

C.

The rabbi of Aleksandrow said that the first time he came to Kotsk, R. Menahem Mendel said to him: I will tell you what is a Hasid. One who constantly asks himself about everything, "What do I want from this?" is a Hasid of Tomaszow. [S.S.K. I:101; E.E. No. 25]

D.

R. Menahem Mendel said: A Hasid is one who rejects the world and one who rejects the world is a Hasid. How is it possible to fulfill both? This is done through the category of "his deed and his hand come simultaneously" [*b. Ked.* 23a]. [S.S.K. I:67; E.E. No. 716]

E.

The rabbi of Pultusk spoke to R. Menahem Mendel about attracting the great scholar, Rabbi Joshua of Kutno. R. Menahem Mendel responded: who chased him away from here? Just because some Hasidim knocked off his hat is no reason to run away. [E.E. No. 142]

[Rabbi Joshua of Kutno was one of the most distinguished scholars and halakhic authorities in Poland at that time. Kotsker Hasidim were notorious for not respecting age, rank or authority. There are many stories of Kotsker Hasidim acting disrespectfully toward important persons. To be humiliated and mocked was a standard form of initiation for anyone coming to Kotsk the first time. It was seen as test to see if one had the right temperament to be a Kotsker Hasid.]

F.

The *Rebbe* of Aleksandrow said about a certain Hasid. In Przysucha they removed his foolishness. In Kotsk, they put him on a firm footing and in Gur they adorned him with spiritual levels. [E.E. No. 825]

24. Hasidic Customs

A.

A disciple of Kotsk once spoke with a Hasid of Chernobyl about their Hasidic customs. He responded that their primary customs were that they stayed up all night on Thursday, and on Friday they contributed to charity according to their ability and on the Sabbath they recited the whole Book of Psalms. R. Menahem Mendel's disciple responded that in Kotsk the order is as follows. They stay up every night and charity is given whenever one encounters a poor person or whenever they have extra funds. They don't have the strength to recite the whole Book of Psalms at one time. King David worshipped God and compiled it over seventy years. They can only recite several Psalms or several verses at a time with *kavannah*. [S.S.K. II:19; E.E. No. 172]

25. Hasidic Practice in Kotsk

A.

"*Beware of going up the mountain or touching the edge*" [Exod 19:12]. If you are going to ascend the mountain, don't suffice with touching the edge, but ascend to the top of the mountain. [E.E. No. 821]

B.

He said: The meaning of "*I exerted myself and did not find, do not believe him*" [*b. Meg.* 6b] is. If you did not find it, don't believe that you exerted yourself. If you had exerted yourself, you would have found what you were seeking. As Scripture says, "*It is not in Heaven, etc.*" [Deut 30:12]. [R.Z., *Elijah Zuta*, ch. 14, 38 n. 3; E.E. No. 62]

C.

He said: The time for eating was youth, and sleeping in the morning. There is no place for depression and he concluded with the following comment. They call this without depression; I call it throwing off the yoke [of heaven]. [S.S.K. I:70; E.E. No. 733]

D.

He was told that it was decided to heat the *mikvah*. He said: Cold *mikvah's* —hot generations; hot *mikvah's*—cold generations. [S.S.K. I:71; E.E. No. 751]

E.

A young man once came to the Kotsker in tears after his wedding. The Kotsker asked him: why are you crying and he responded that he had just gotten married and his father-in-law had not given him a *talit*. He told him: one wraps oneself with the four corners of the earth. [S.S.K. IV:118; E.E. No. 130]

[It was the custom in Eastern Europe that one did not wear a *talit* until one married and it was also customary that the groom received this as a present from his father-in-law. One of the names for a *talit katan* that is worn under the shirt is *arba kanfot* (four corners).]

F.

One who can show himself a "fig"[4] can do the same to the whole world. [E.E. No. 133]

G.

R. Samuel of Sochaczew said: My grandfather, the Kotsker said that the whole world isn't even worth that someone should give one groan over it. [A.R. No. 216; E.E. No. 337]

---

4. A sign of disrespect. It is indicated by holding the thumb between the first two fingers while making a fist.

H.

He once said in public. I only want three things from them [his disciples]. Not to look outside of oneself, not to look into another person, and not to mean oneself. This is the foundation of being a Jew. [S.S.K. I:68; E.E. No. 720]

["Not to mean oneself" is another way of saying, not to be self-centered. Not being self-centered is the common motif in all of these sayings.]

26. Heart

A.

The *zaddiq* of Kotsk said about the verse, "*these things that I command you should be on your heart*" [Deut 6:6]. It is not written, in your heart. Sometimes the heart is closed and the words will rest, like a heavy stone, on the heart. When the heart will open in a sacred moment, the words will fall into the depths of the heart. [R.Z., *Elijah Zuta*, ch. 15, 43 n. 26; S.S.K. IV:55; E.E. No. 887][5]

B.

"*Impress these My words upon your very heart*" [Deut 11:18]. This thing should lie like a stone on your heart. [R.Z., *Elijah Zuta*, ch. 15, 43 n. 25]

C.

R. Menahem Mendel was careful never to wear a scarf during the times of prayer so that he should not cause a disruption between the mind and the heart. [E.E. No. 846]

[Similarly, the "*gartel*" the silk belt worn by Hasidim during prayer is a symbolic garment of separation between the lower part of the body that is seen as being essentially physical and the upper part that is seen as being more spiritual.]

---

5. S.S.K. IV:54–55 contains another version of this saying from a different source.

27. Holiness

A.

"*Let them make me a sanctuary that I may dwell among them*" [Exod 25:8]. That is, each person should make within himself a place of holiness where the *Shekhinah* can dwell. [S.S.K. III:24–25; E.E. No. 157]

B.

It is written, "*You shall be holy*" [Lev 19:2]. How can a human being be holy? Because it is written, "*I, the Lord your God, am holy*" [Lev 19:2]. [L.T. 427 n. 41; E.E. No. 250]

C.

"*You shall be holy, for I your Lord am holy*" [Lev 19:2]. Holiness is a term of invitation; that you should all be prepared to receive. "*For I your Lord am holy*" and am always ready to save you; only that you should be prepared with holy thoughts. [E.E. No. 427]

D.

There is holiness in deeds and there is holiness in the mind. [E.E. No. 251]

E.

He once said to a groom who came for a blessing before his wedding. Why did the Talmudic sages choose the language "you are sanctified unto me" and not some of the other possible phrases like, "you are betrothed to me" or "you will be my wife" [*b. Ked.* 6a]? They alluded with these words that a person needs to enter this matter with holiness and purity. If not, then the deepest hell is not enough for him, heaven forbid. [E.E. No. 11]

F.

It says, "*The Lord your God will circumcise your heart*" [Deut 30:6]. Earlier in Deuteronomy it says, "*circumcise the foreskin of your heart*" [Deut 10:16]. This implies that the person is obligated to remove the foreskin of his heart. In truth, the person is obligated to remove the covering of his heart by himself, so that his heart will be ready to receive the holiness into it. However, that his heart should be transformed from one extreme to the other, that he should have no desires at all, is not in the hand of the person. This is only possible if God will circumcise his heart. That is why it first says, *"the foreskin of your heart,"* and then it says, *"The Lord your God will circumcise your heart."* [E.E. No. 515]

G.

One of R. Menahem Mendel's grandchildren said that he saw the following written in a *humash* in Sochaczew. R. Menahem Mendel said: The Torah portion *Kedoshim* [Lev 19:1–20:27] begins with *"You shall be holy"* and ends with *"their blood is upon them."* It should cost blood, but one should be holy. [E.E. No. 812]

H.

"You shall be holy" [Lev 19:2]. It should not appear to the person that he has fulfilled his obligation and that he has on what to stand and this is something like I can do. The Talmudic sages say [*Lev. Rab.* 19:2]: "Because I am holy. My holiness is above your holiness." This is because whatever you sanctify yourself, you need to recognize that My holiness is higher and you still have not fulfilled your obligation. It is like someone who walks into the king's courtyard and is afraid. When he enters the house, his fear is greater. As he goes further in, the fear gets greater. So too is it with a person who sanctifies himself and approaches the truth. The closer he approaches, the greater his fear. [E.E. No. 875]

I.

Whoever sanctifies himself below is also sanctified by Heaven. [E.E. No. 897]

28. Honor

A.

R. Menahem Mendel used to compare the three things in tractate *Avot*, envy, lust and honor[6] to three inns that are scattered among the villages on the road that a person travels from city to city. He said that he never had much interest in the first two inns, but at the last inn, that of honor, he had a lot of work to do, and not with worldly honor. The first time he came to visit the Seer of Lublin, he was still a young man and the Seer honored him greatly. In the morning, he invited him to pray with the holy company of great scholars that prayed with the Seer. He had to work for a number of years to in order to be able to get that honor out from between his teeth. [A.R. No. 68; E.E. No. 401]

29. Humility

A.

"*And he put a veil over his face*" [Exod 34:33]. The meaning is not that Moses put a mask on his face, but that he hid himself in his inwardness. [E.E. No. 89]

B.

"*And the man Moses was very humble*" [Num 12:3]. Rashi comments: lowly and long suffering. That is, he suffered the lowliness. [E.E. No. 460]

C.

R. Menahem Mendel told R. Hirsch Tomaszower that he should exert himself on behalf of R. Ze'ev Nahum of Biala, his daughter's father-in-law that he should receive the rabbinical post in Biala. The matter was successful and when he came to Kotsk, he said to R. Menahem Mendel, I have been appointed rabbi of Biala. R. Menahem Mendel said to him in a loud voice. You've been appointed rabbi in Biala? How courageous of you. With what merit are you worthy of this? The rabbi of Biala was very confused and left

---

6. *m. Avot* 4.21. "Envy, lust, and honor are three things that take a man out of the world."

the room very embittered. A short while later, Feivel the *shamash,* came and told him that R. Menahem Mendel was calling him. He went in broken hearted. R. Menahem Mendel said to him warmly, you've been appointed rabbi in Biala, congratulations. May you be successful there. [E.E. No. 656]

D.

R. Menahem Mendel said that the purpose of the frame around the first word of every Talmudic tractate is that when a person sits down to study he needs to hide himself inside the word so that people would not see him. [E.E. No. 850]

E.

"*Man has no superiority over beast, since both amount to nothing*" [Eccl 3:19]. This is the advantage of the person over the beast, that in his own eyes he is in the category of nothing. [E.E. No. 213]

[Humanity is superior to the animal because they have the consciousness of being nothing. Humility is the essence of humanity.]

30. Impurity

A.

Impurity comes from the power of the Evil Side, and its tendency is to attach itself to the place of importance, that which comes from holiness. That is why it was considered a miracle that a fly was not seen in the Temple's kitchens. [*m. Avot* 5.5] A fly refers to the evil inclination. The miracle was that the powers of impurity could not attach themselves to the Temple. Also, a fly was not seen on Elisha's table. Therefore, the significance of a clay vessel is its interior and only it can become impure and not it's exterior. [E.E. No. 508]

B.

"*If any of these falls into an earthen vessel, etc. you shall break it*" [Lev 11:33]. R. Menahem Mendel of Kotsk said: what is the reason that it only becomes impure on the inside and can't be purified in the *mikveh*? The reason is that its only value is its ability to contain something. Therefore, only its interior can become impure. The person is similar; understand this. [N.H 82; O.T. 56; S.S.K. IV:19]

31. Integrity

A.

R. Isaac Meir said that R. Menahem Mendel once said. I don't know what they want from me. All week they do what they want. When the holy Sabbath comes, they put on a black coat, a black *gartel,* a black *shtreimel* and they are immediately in-laws of the *Lecha Dodi.*[7] I say: "your deeds during the week should be like your deeds on the Sabbath." [*b. Sukkah* 45a] [E.E. No. 882]

32. Isaac of Warka

A.

When they were still in Przysucha, R. Menahem Mendel once went with R. Isaac of Warka to Przysucha. They needed a small knife. An old woman was standing there with knives. Isaac went over to her and asked about the price. She said: four pennies. He responded that he would only give her three. R. Menahem Mendel shouted at him: Isaac, "don't talk excessively with a woman" [*m. Avot* 1.5], is also worth a penny. [E.E. No. 451]

[Though they differed significantly, R. Menahem Mendel and R. Isaac were close friends since the time they were disciples of R. Simhah Bunem. The warmth of their relationship comes through in many of these passages.]

B.

R. Jacob David of Amshinov was once visiting R. Menahem Mendel after the death of his father, R. Isaac of Warka. He admitted to him that he had not seen his father in his dreams after his father's death. R. Menahem

7. *Lecha Dodi* is a hymn addressed to the *Shekhinah,* the Sabbath Queen, sung on Friday evening at the beginning of the Sabbath. It marks the transition from weekday to Sabbath. To be "in-laws" is a Yiddish expression meaning, to be on close terms with someone or something.

Mendel said that he will see him and while he was still in Kotsk, he saw him. He told R. Menahem Mendel that he had seen him and R. Menahem Mendel asked, in what situation had he seen him. He responded that he saw him standing near a river, leaning on his staff, and looking at the river. R. Menahem Mendel said: do you know what this river is? This is the river of the tears of Israel. When we were disciples of R. Simhah Bunem of Przysucha, he said that he would place one disciple to oppose his opponents and enemies and he would be like R. Elimelech of Lyzhansk. At first I thought that R. Simhah Bunem's reference was to me, but later I realized that the reference was to your father. [E.E. No. 740]

C.

R. Menahem Mendel followed the path of seclusion, while the path of his friend, R. Isaac of Warka was that of associating with his Hasidim. They once met and R. Menahem Mendel said; my path is alluded to in the Torah, in the words "*they should take for me*" [Exod 25:2]. If someone wants the path of truth, it is as Rashi comments, "*for me*" means, for my Name. The advice of "*terumah*" is to separate from people, even the good ones.[8] Even from "*every man who would donate his heart*" [Exod 25:2]. R. Isaac of Warka said, my path also is from this verse, "*they should take for me a donation [terumah]*" [Exod 25:2], from each one of them, to associate with them and to learn from them. [E.E. No. 799]

D.

R. Menahem Mendel once traveled to Przysucha on the *yahrzeit* of R. Simhah Bunem of Przysucha. R. Isaac of Warka was there and he said to him, "Isaac, I didn't come for the memorial observances. I'm not a cemetery visitor. I only came to see you." [E.E. No. 123]

E.

When R. Menahem Mendel came to Przysucha, to the grave of R. Simhah Bunem on the first anniversary of the death, he said to R. Isaac of Warka. You know that I don't come to cry on graves, but I have come to discuss

---

8. This is a play on the word "*terumah*" which means to contribute and to separate something as a holy offering.

a proposal with you. The rabbi of Warka responded: I don't worry about people who spend their days in the *bet midrash*. I worry about the Jew in the marketplace. [E.E. No. 855]

F.

R. Menahem Mendel asked R. Isaac of Warka what he saw in Chernobyl. He said that he saw the table of the Baal Shem Tov. R. Menahem Mendel said: you saw a table that is about one hundred years old. However, our *Rebbe* [R. Simhah Bunem of Przysucha] always shows us things that are almost six thousand years old, which are the heavens and earth, and who created them. [E.E. No. 171]

G.

The bride and groom stood under the wedding canopy for a long time along with all the dignitaries for a long time and it was very cold. After a long time, R. Menahem Mendel came out and greeted everyone pleasantly. Afterwards, he said to R. Isaac Meir of Gur and his son David: You were surely surprised why I did not come to the wedding ceremony immediately. I have to tell you the reason for this. I had invited my dear friend, R. Isaac of Warka, of blessed memory, to come to my celebration and he came before the ceremony. How could I leave my room as long as such a dear friend was with me? [E.E. No. 275]

H.

R. Menahem Mendel was once told that R. Isaac of Warka told that it is found in the *Zohar* [I:117a] "*in the year 5600, the fountains of wisdom will be opened.*" And so it was. However, since Israel was not worthy of it, the wisdom was transmitted to others. As the result of this many new things were invented and scientific discoveries were made. R. Menahem Mendel became angry and said to the person who told him this: you had such pearls of wisdom in your hand and you have been here several days and you did not tell me this. [E.E. No. 263]

[This passage from the *Zohar* was widely quoted during this period. It was also seen as a reference to the beginning of the Messianic Age. Israel was not worthy to be redeemed by the Messiah, so the fountains of wisdom spilled into secular and worldly knowledge.[9]]

33. Joy

A.

"*Because you would not serve the Lord your God with joy, etc.*" [Deut 28:47]. Is it because of this that they deserve all the chastisements? Rather, the issue is that they did not worship with joy but as "*a commandment of men learned by rote*" [Isa 29:13]. The person's ardor cooled off and he forgot that there is a Creator of the world and he committed all the transgressions that came to hand. Therefore he is punished with all the punishments enumerated. When the person will examine the reason for the transgressions, he will see that all these punishments happened as a result of his not worshiping God with joy. [E.E. No. 514]

B.

R. Menahem Mendel said that it would be a great joy to be killed by a *Bet Din*, because his death would be according to the Torah. [E.E. No. 747]

C.

"*You will leave in joy*" [Isa 55:12]. The meaning is, with joy you will be able to leave all troubles. [E.E. No. 804]

D.

Joy is the expansion of holiness. Therefore, the festival of *Sukkot* that comes after *Yom Kippur*, the time of forgiveness of sins, is called the time of our rejoicing. [L.T. 427 n. 37; E.E. No. 244, No. 784]

9. See Morgenstern, "Messianic Expectations for the year 5600 (1840)"

34. Kabbalistic Customs

A.

A Habad Hasid once came to Kotsk and asked R. Menahem Mendel which mystical intention [*kavvanah*] he concentrated on during the *Shema* and the *Amidah*. R. Menahem Mendel shouted in a loud voice, "and where is the navel [*pupik*]?" [S.S.K. IV:21; E.E. No. 80]

[The *"pupik"* (navel) is a term for the "gut," the emotional center.]

B.

A *mitnaged* asked R. Menahem Mendel when was the hour of *tikkun hazot* for him, since he saw that R. Menahem Mendel stayed up until midnight and then had his evening meal. He responded that when he recited "*Rebuild Jerusalem*" in the Grace after meals, was the time of *tikkun hazot* for him. [S.S.K. II:25; E.E. No. 188]

[*Tikkun hazot* is a kabbalistic ritual that is performed after midnight. A central part of it is mourning for the destruction and praying for the restoration of the Temple. R. Menahem Mendel's flippant response is in line with the general lack of interest in kabbalistic matters in the Przysucha-Kotsk School.]

C.

R. Menahem Mendel said: a Jew without a *gartel* is like a barrel without hoops. [E.E. No. 800]

35. Leadership

A.

He said about his teacher, R. Simhah Bunem of Przysucha. He raised and helped all who sought refuge in his shadow. However, he wanted that each person should raise himself. [E.E. No. 21]

B.

R. Isaac Meir of Gur said: R. Simhah Bunem led his followers with love. R. Menahem Mendel led them with fear and awe. I lead them with Torah [scholarship]. [E.E. No. 272]

C.

"*Let the Lord appoint someone over the community*" [Num 27:16]. Moses thought that God would appoint Phinehas as leader, but He did not want this because Phinehas was impatient. [E.E. No. 475; 861]

36. R. Menahem Mendel on Himself

A.

He said that he became a Hasid through an old man who told stories about the holy *zaddiqim*. He put it this way: "He told and I heard." [S.S.K. I:72; E.E. No. 753]

B.

R. Menahem Mendel once said loudly to someone. Do you know who I am? There was R. Baer of Mezhirech, R. Shmelke of Nikolsburg, R. Elimelech of Lyzhansk, The Seer of Lublin, the Holy Yehudi, R. Simhah Bunem, and I am the seventh, the quintessence of all of them. I am the Sabbath. [E.E. No. 906]

C.

R. Menahem Mendel said: I can revive the dead, but I would rather revive the living. [E.E. No. 901]

D.

R. Menahem Mendel once said about himself that his soul was from the souls that existed before the destruction of the Temple. He said: I have only come now to this world to clarify what is holy and what is external [to holiness]. [A.R. No. 49; E.E. No. 377]

68

E.

When he was a young child, R. Menahem Mendel had an argument with his teacher. He said: You are arguing with me? I remember when I stood at Mount Sinai when God said *"I am the Lord your God"* [Exod 20:20]. [E.E. No. 786]

F.

The author of the *Shem Mi-Shmuel*,[10] said that his grandfather, the Kotsker, said that he could make the whole world Hasidim, but this would not be good. [S.S.K. IV:56; E.E. No. 105]

G.

I have no reason to examine my ancestry. The Maggid of Kozienice said that if he knew for certain that he was descended from Abraham, Isaac, and Jacob, he would put his hat aside and dance a "kazatski"[11] in the middle of the marketplace. Indeed, I know for certain that my descent is from Abraham, Isaac, and Jacob. [E.E. No. 94]

H.

R. Menahem Mendel once said about himself. "I have one foot in the seventh heaven and one in the deepest hell." [S.S.K. III:19–20]

I.

R. Menahem Mendel told that in his youth there was a decree in his country that one could not marry until one had learned the language of the country. Therefore, it was the custom to teach young children the language. He also learned it, but was careful that it should not harm him. [E.E. No. 261]

[This was a decree of the Austro-Hungarian Empire, as part of their efforts to "modernize" the Jews.]

---

10. A commentary on the Torah and Hasidic teachings by R. Samuel of Sochaczew.
11. A Cossack-style dance.

J.

R. Menahem Mendel said to the Rabbi of Aleksandrow. If he did not have to speak with people he would not have needed to eat, since the life force of the holy Torah would be enough for him. R. Menahem Mendel asked if the same was true for him. [E.E. No. 286]

K.

R. Simhah Bunem once said to his disciple, R. Menahem Mendel of Tomaszow. If it turns out that I have to go to Gehenna, what should I do? R. Menahem Mendel did not respond. After a few moments, R. Simhah Bunem said: This is what I will do. I will command that they bring the Rabbi of Lublin of blessed memory, and the Yehudi of Przysucha of blessed memory. As the Talmudic sages said, "a disciple who is exiled, his teacher is exiled with him" [*b. Mak.* 10a]. R. Menahem Mendel then said: It won't matter for his honor, but it will be useful for me. [E.E. No. 320]

L.

On 11 *Ellul*, 1827 R. Menahem Mendel traveled with his son David to Opazna for his son's wedding. He received permission for this from his teacher, R. Simhah Bunem of blessed memory. He asked if he should travel to his son's wedding since his teacher was ill. He told him to go. On 12 *Ellul* R. Simhah Bunem died and R. Menahem Mendel came to Przysucha on 13 *Ellul* after the funeral of R. Simhah Bunem. He asked to be given the key to the room where R. Simhah Bunem had died. They gave it to him and he locked himself in the room. When he came out, he said, none of you were at his funeral except for me. [E.E. No. 330]

M.

R. Menahem Mendel said: the soul, even if it is in the mountains of darkness, must come to him in Kotsk for a repair [*tikkun*]. [E.E. No. 334]

["Mountains of darkness" is an expression meaning "the ends of the earth".]

N.

He once said: If you will listen to me, it will be good. If not, I will don a mask of fear and you will run away into the mouse holes. [L.T. 428 n. 49; E.E. No. 253]

O.

R. Menahem Mendel said about himself that he does not need the help of angels to raise up his prayers, since his prayers always ascend directly. "They don't know what they possess." [E.E. No. 378]

37. R. Menahem Mendel's Seclusion

A.

During the twenty years that he was in seclusion in his private room, he did not come to the table to celebrate in public on Sabbaths and Festivals. Occasionally, he would open the door of his room before the assembled group, dressed in shirtsleeves and *talit katan*, without his jacket, and his appearance was awesome, like an angel of the Lord. He spoke a few words in a loud voice and his rebukes hit the gut and a great fear fell upon the assembled group and they ran outside. [E.E. No. 264]

B.

His important disciples were once seated at a table. He opened the door of his room and shouted the following verse at them. "*Like a bear robbed of her young I attack them and rip open the casing of their hearts*" [Hos 13:8]. They all ran away out of fear. [E.E. No. 760]

C.

During the period of seclusion, R. Isaac Meir of Gur came with his son. The *shamash*, Feivel, entered to announce that R. Isaac Meir had arrived. Several hours later, R. Isaac Meir entered with his son and stayed for a period of time. After they left, R. Menahem Mendel called Feivel and shouted at him, "why did you not tell me about the arrival of R. Isaac Meir. Feivel excused himself and said that he thought that mentioning his arrival was sufficient.

R. Menahem Mendel responded, "an in-law is something special." For an in-law one has to put on other clothes. [E.E. No. 274]

38. Messiah/ Messianic Age

A.

"*The Lord said to Moses: Why do you cry out to me?*" [Exod 14:15]. The commentaries ask: To whom should one call out to in a time of trouble, if not God? Someone came to R. Menahem Mendel of Kotsk and R. Menahem Mendel asked him, which *zaddiq* did he normally visit? He said that he normally visited the holy R. Solomon Leib [of Leczna], of blessed memory. [R. Menahem Mendel said.] I loved him very much, and now he cries out to God every day that He should bring the Messiah. The explanation is that R. Solomon cries out to God that he should bring the Messiah, but God wants that the Messiah should come. The essential thing is that he should cry out to the children of Israel that they should repent and the Messiah will certainly come. The Holy One said the same thing to Moses. Why do you cry out to me? Rather, speak to the children of Israel and let them leave their previous thoughts, when they said, "*are there not enough graves in Egypt?*" [Exod 14:11], when they wanted to return to Egypt, when they lost their faith. Let them strengthen their faith and they will be helped quickly. [N.H. 61]

B.

One of the disciples of R. Solomon Leib of Leczna once visited R. Menahem Mendel, who asked him, how is your *Rebbe*? I love him very much, but why does he shout to God to send the Messiah? Why does he not shout to Israel that they should repent? This is the meaning of "*Why do you cry out to Me? Tell the Israelites to go forward*" [Exod 14:15]. [E.E. No. 702]

C.

A Hasid told that he heard how R. Menahem Mendel was talking about how the *Geonim* wanted to bring the Messiah in one way, but could not succeed. Then the Tosafists tried to bring the Messiah, but could not succeed. Then the *Posekim* also wanted to bring the Messiah, but could not succeed. Then the preachers of rebuke and the *zaddiqim* wanted to bring the Messiah in a different manner, but could not succeed.[12] He concluded and said: the Messiah will come when the minds of the children of Israel will be preoccupied with worries about livelihood and their thought will be confused, then the Messiah will come in a moment. [S.S.K. IV:113; E.E. No. 129]

D.

In the book *Avkat Rokhel*,[13] the author exaggerated the tribulations preceding the advent of the messianic age. R. Menahem Mendel said about this: indeed, the author has to do the will of God, but God does not have to do the will of the author. [E.E. No. 305]

E.

R. Menahem Mendel said: During the birth pangs of the Messiah,[14] even great *zaddiqim* will need mercy so that they don't fall into heresy, heaven forbid. [S.S.K. IV:106; E.E. No. 125]

39. Miracles

A.

In the Torah portion, *"these are the journeys of the children of Israel"* [Num 33:1], not only are written the journeys of the children of Israel who left Egypt, but they also include all the miracles that are done for Israel in all their exiles. However, no person understands what is written. Therefore, it is written, *""who alone works great marvels"* [Ps 136:4]. The only one who understands them is the Holy One and they are written in Heaven. All the events of the exile continue to be written in Heaven and in the future, a special book will be written about them. [E.E. No. 258; E.E. No. 619]

---

12. This list is a shorthand way of saying all the great religious worthies of Jewish history.

13. Attributed to R. Judah the son of R. Asher of Barcelona.

14. The period immediately preceding the coming of the Messiah.

40. Modesty

A.

The Midrash says: the first Tablets were given publicly and therefore the evil eye ruled over them and they were broken. Here[15] God says: there is nothing nicer than modesty. [Midrash *Tanh. Ki Tisa* 31] The meaning of the first Tablets were given publicly is that the holiness of Israel was the result of God sanctifying them more than they sanctified themselves and that is why the Tablets did not last, in their hands. That which does not come from the person's own exertion does not last. Therefore, it was desired that the second tablets should be from their side, that they should sanctify themselves more through this, since there is nothing nicer than modesty, as Scripture says, "*What does the Lord require of you . . . to walk modestly . . .*" [Mic 6:8]. [E.E. No. 411]

41. Money

A.

The *zaddiq*, R. Feivel of Gryce, told that he was once talking with R. Menahem Mendel about money. R. Menahem Mendel responded with disgust. What did you say, money? I despise it. These words weighed on the heart of the *zaddiq*, R. Feivel, until in a number of months money was so disgusting in his eyes that he could not even look at it. [L.T. 428 n. 44; E.E. No. 122]

B.

There was one Hasid who used to support R. Menahem Mendel financially, since he would not take money from anyone else. One time he did not want to take money from him and he asked R. Menahem Mendel about this. He responded, for every income there is a reason. If God wants to test a person then He takes away the reason. If one trusts in the reason then his income is taken away from him, but if he trusts in God despite the reasons, then his income is restored. Thus, the reason for my income is that you fund me. It occurred to me. Perhaps God wants to test me and take away the reason and you will be forced to be poor, in order not to fund me. The Hasid responded: If so, if the Holy One wants to test our master and will make me

---

15. Regarding the second set of Tablets.

74

poor, I will accept it. He implored R. Menahem Mendel and he accepted money from him. He became poor, may it not happen to us, and had to accept a rabbinical position in another city. [S.S.K. I:74; E.E. No. 769]

42. Movement in Worship

A.

The rabbi of Sochaczew once told that in his youth he was weak and coughed up blood. On *Rosh Hashanah*, R. Menahem Mendel took him in to pray with him in his private room near the large *bet midrash*. He saw him pray the *Amidah* and listen to the shofar blasts without any movement or external expression, but his face glowed like a torch. [E.E. No. 256]

[Menahem Mendel's negative attitude toward movement in worship is in sharp contrast to the prevailing Hasidic tradition. There are numerous stories of Hasidic *zaddiqim* beginning with the Baal Shem Tov who engaged in extreme movements during prayer. It is told of several *zaddiqim* that they would begin their prayers in one corner and wind up in the opposite side of the room by the time they finished their prayers.]

B.

In *parshat Beha'alotekha* it is written: "*Aaron did so*" [Num 8:3]. Rashi comments: "This is to praise Aaron, that he did not change anything."[16] He did not make any external movements, but everything was within his heart. The external movements are not so important, but the important thing is that it should be hidden and embedded in his heart. Similarly, he understands the verse, "*they fell back and stood at a distance . . . Moses approached the thick cloud . . .*" [Exod 20:15–18]. That is, "*they fell back,*" they made external movements with their bodies and because of this, "*stood at a distance.*" However, Moses approached the thick cloud without any movement. [E.E. No. 149, E.E. No. 494]

C.

"*The people saw, they fell back and stood at a distance*" [Exod 20:15–18]. One can see, one can sway back and forth, and yet be distant. [E.E. No. 870].

16. Rashi on Num 8:3.

D.

"*If you remove your abominations from my presence and do not waver*" [Jer 4:1]. The reason that people sway back and forth [*shokel*] during prayer is because they are burdened with unpleasant thoughts. Therefore, they strengthen themselves against them through these movements. However, "*if you remove your abominations*," if you remove the filth from your thoughts, then you will have no need to move your body. [S.S.K. II:87; E.E. No. 196]

43. Music

A.

"*As the musician played, the hand of God came upon him*" [2 Kgs 3:15]. R. Menahem Mendel said: whoever is a proper musician and has no ulterior motives can bring the redemption closer, because the Palace of song is close to the Palace of the Messiah. Thus, when the musician plays and has no ulterior motive, then the hand of God will be upon him. [N.H. 147; E.E. No. 536]

44. Opinion of Others

A.

"*We looked like grasshoppers to ourselves and that is how we must have looked to them*" [Num 13:33]. This is difficult. When it says, "*we looked like grasshoppers to ourselves*," that is still possible to understand. However, "*that is how we must have looked to them*"; what do you care what you look like in the eyes of others? [E.E. No. 496]

B.

One should always suspect what people are saying. The proof for this is from the verse "*and the eyes of Leah were weak*" [Gen 29:17]. She cried because people said that she would marry Esau.[17] Who was saying this, Laban and his contemporaries? Why should she cry about this? Rather one should suspect what people say. [E.E. No. 809]

---

17. This interpretation is based on *Gen. Rab.* 70.16.

45. Others on R. Menahem Mendel

A.

After the death of R. Simhah Bunem of Przysucha, his leading disciples gathered for an advisory meeting. Many of those gathered looked to one special disciple, R. Menahem Mendel, then living in Tomaszow. All of them knew how valued he was by their teacher, of blessed memory, and that he meticulously followed his teacher and his practices. There were some Hasidim who had a different opinion, because of the persecutions of Przysucha Hasidim that had been partially caused by R. Menahem Mendel. His spiritual path was a spark of fire, a flame of holiness that burned within him that did not defer to any person, not even the most important. [E.E. No. 790]

[Other Hasidic groups viewed Przysucha Hasidism negatively and disdained their perceived radicalism. Among the Przysucha disciples most often cited for his radicalism was R. Menahem Mendel. The controversy was brought to a head at a famous wedding in the town of Ustilag, where the opponents of Przysucha tried to have them excommunicated. After much discussion, the excommunication was narrowly averted. Nonetheless, the distrust continued, especially after the accession of R. Menahem Mendel to the leadership.]

B.

The Rabbi of Lublin once asked the Yehudi of Przysucha if he had any young men who were good. He responded that Mendel of Tomaszow desires to have fear of Heaven. R. Menahem Mendel said in his old age, I still didn't want it then, but from then on I desired it and still desire it. [*Niflaot ha-Yehudi*, 53; E.E. No. 798]

C.

R. Hirsch Tomaszower said; I can testify that until his last moment the *Rebbe* of Kotsk worked on the teachings of Judaism with the enthusiasm of a young man who is just beginning his study of Judaism. [E.E. 139]

D.

The rabbi of Sochaczew said: I have seen many *Rebbes*, but my father-in-law, of blessed memory, of Kotsk was literally an angel of the Lord of Hosts. [E.E. No. 408]

E.

The *zaddiq*, the author of the *Sefat Emet*,[18] said about R. Menahem Mendel in these words: Whatever you will say about him, he was an angel who walked in this world. [E.E. No. 259]

F.

When news reached Warsaw that R. Menahem Mendel's medical condition had worsened, R. Isaac Meir began to tell great and wondrous praises about him, that there was never found a true Jew like him and he said that according to his opinion, his stature was as great as that of the Baal Shem Tov. [E.E. No. 280]

G.

The Rabbi of Aleksandrow said that there are three commentaries on R. Simhah Bunem. The first commentary is that of R. Menahem Mendel, the second of R. Isaac Meir of Gur, and others. [E.E. No. 332]

H.

The Rabbi of Sochaczew said about R. Menahem Mendel: It is certain that the Messiah would not implant Judaism in the heart of every Jew more than was implanted by R. Menahem Mendel. [E.E. No. 333]

I.

When R. Menahem Mendel's reputation began to spread, a householder in the town of Goray, in the province of Tomaszow head about this and was very surprised he would be a *Rebbe*. I studied with him together in

18. Yehudah Leib of Gur, the author of the *Sefat Emet*, was the grandson of Isaac Meir of Gur, his closest disciple.

the same class when we were children. The Hasidim then began to ask him about R. Menahem Mendel's practices when he was a child. He said that he doesn't know anything, except for one time; the teacher went with the students on Lag Be-Omer to the mountains. When they returned, they discovered that Menahem Mendel was not with them. They went back to look for him and they saw him lying on the ground, with his hands and feet spread out and heard him reciting the verse, "*my body and soul shout for joy to the living God*" [Ps 84:3]. [E.E. No. 668]

J.

When R. Hayyim of Plonsk left Przysucha to become the rabbi of New Ciechanowi, the Lithuanian scholars asked him about the intellectual level of the group in Przysucha. He responded: R. Isaac of Warka is learned, R. Isaac Meir of Gur is a genius, and his colleagues cannot plumb the intellectual depths of the rabbi of Tomaszow. [E.E. No. 694]

K.

The rabbi of Radzymin said that the key to healing barren women is found by R. Menahem Mendel. [E.E. No. 705]

[This is a rather unusual compliment. His other disciples praised his intellectual powers. Here, he is praising his magical abilities, something not normally associated with Kotsk. However, see, below, the section on "The *Zaddiq* and His Powers."]

L.

R. Menahem Mendel studied the teachings of Maimonides diligently. [E.E. No. 710]

M.

R. Isaiah of Praga said that R. Isaac Meir once said to him that ninety-nine percent of the reason that he traveled to Przysucha was because he knew that R. Menahem Mendel was there and he wanted to see him and talk with him. [E.E. No. 794]

N.

R. Hanokh of Aleksandrow said: I was once visiting R. Menahem Mendel of Kotsk and I asked him. What should I do so that I should have desire to study. He was very surprised. How is it possible that someone should not desire such a good thing? Then he said that I should study with more devotion. [E.E. No. 913]

46. Penitents [ba'ale teshuvah]

A.

"In the place where penitents [ba'ale teshuvah] stand, even totally righteous people [zaddiqim gemurim] cannot stand" [b. Ber. 34b]. This is like a merchant who buys merchandise with a great deal of effort; he will certainly not sell it cheaply. However, someone who buys merchandise easily can sell it cheaply, since he did not exert himself for it. This is the meaning of "in the place where penitents stand." That is, the penitent can accept whatever reward he is given in return for his work, since he did not work hard for it. However, the completely righteous person who was worked hard from the day he is born cannot accept a reward like this. [E.E. No. 585]

47. Piety

A.

Someone asked him: What is wrong with people calling him pious? He responded that the pious one makes what is secondary primary and what is primary secondary. [S.S.K. I:75; E.E. No. 770]

[Piety was not in itself important in Kotsk. Spiritual struggle and growth, the process of attaining piety, was more important.]

B.

"Fear of sin leads to piety [Hasidut]" [b. Avod. Zar. 20b]. There are a number of steps until one gets to piety, so how do we call someone a pietist if he has not traversed all the steps? There are small paths that distinguished individuals find in order in order to come to piety immediately. However, if everyone would go on this path, it would become damaged and they would have to take the path of the steps. [E.E. No. 599]

48. Prayer

A.

A Hasid once came to him and spoke of his spiritual distress and financial worries. He responded that he should pray with his whole heart and soul to God and the Merciful One will surely have mercy on him. The Hasid responded that he did not know how to pray by himself to the Great and Awesome King, the Ruler of the World, the Holy One. R. Menahem Mendel told him. If so, you have a greater worry than financial problems, you don't know how to pray. [S.S.K. I:68; E.E. No. 722]

B.

R. Hirsch Parszewer was the cantor for the High Holy Days in Przysucha, Kotsk and later in Gur. Once there was a great fire and everything Hirsch owned was destroyed. He came to his teacher, R. Menahem Mendel, and told him about his loss. He responded that this had happened because he had repeated the words "who by fire" in the piyyut, U-Netane Tokef.[19] The voice of R. Menahem Mendel was often heard in the bet midrash when a prayer was repeated, as was customary, saying, "Hirsch, shorten it." [S.S.K. II:26; E.E. No. 737]

C.

The shofar blower thought that he did not blow one blast properly, so he blew it again. R. Menahem Mendel said to him: one doesn't regrind the blast. [E.E. No. 206]

[These two (B. and C.) are examples of the Kotsker disapproval of excessive outward piety. One fulfills the religious obligation, but does not overdo it.]

---

19. A central prayer in the liturgy of Rosh Hashanah and Yom Kippur.

D.

A rich man once came to R. Menahem Mendel because he had no children. R. Menahem Mendel kept putting him off until ten years had passed. Finally after ten years he ordered him to give his wife a divorce. When he came home, after an absence of three months, he saw that his wife was pregnant. He was concerned that the child might be someone else's and he returned a second time to Kotsk. R. Menahem Mendel said to him. Make the circumcision; the child is yours. He continued: know that you were infertile, but on your way home you prayed with a broken heart at the place where R. Simhah Bunem had stayed on his way home before his wedding, and this helped you. [E.E. No. 856]

E.

One of his most distinguished disciples once told R. Menahem Mendel that on a number of occasions he did not feel *devekut* or heartfelt pleasure during his prayers, and what are they worth without the proper intentions? R. Menahem Mendel responded that this should not trouble him at all. The virtue of prayer is so great that if one prays once with some proper intentions that prayer will drag along with it and raise up before the Heavenly Throne all those prayers that did not have the proper intentions. They all ascend in one group, full and complete, to the Heavenly Throne. [E.E. No. 8]

F.

"*Cross over and see*" [Deut 3:25]. When you will cross over you will certainly see. However, his prayer should also be on the seeing. When a person is engaged in something also needs to pray to God that he will see the good in that matter. [E.E. No. 482]

G.

In Midrash *Tanhuma, Ki Tavo* 1, it says: Moses looked into the future with divine inspiration and saw that the Temple would be destroyed. He rose and ordained that Israel should pray three times a day, every day. It seems that when he saw that the offering of the First Fruits would be abrogated in the future, he reflected that they are not an essential matter, since an essential thing would not be abrogated. Therefore, he ordained prayer, since it is found in all times without abrogation. [E.E. No. 513]

H.

"The ancient pietists would reflect for an hour and pray in order that they should incline their hearts to their Heavenly Father" [*b. Ber.* 30b]. It should be, and afterwards they would pray. However, the meaning is, they would reflect for an hour and pray during that hour that they should incline their hearts afterwards. [E.E. No. 584]

I.

R. Menahem Mendel once called R. Hirsch Parszewer on the eve of *Yom Kippur* and said to him. I am appointing you as the prayer leader for the Jews who cannot pray, for the Jews in the fields around here, not only the living, but also the dead. You should know that the walls are covered with souls. [E.E. No. 844]

J.

"*And angels of the Lord encountered him*" [Gen 32:2]. "Encounter is a term for prayer" [*b. Ber.* 26b]. Whoever walks in the path of Torah, even angels of the Lord, that is, angels of judgment, ask for mercy on his behalf. [E.E. No. 313]

49. Prophecy/Prophetic Powers

A.

"A wise man is preferable to a prophet" [*b. B. Bat.* 12a]. Wisdom is a form of prophecy. [S.S.K. II:93; E.E. No. 204]

B.

The *Rebbe* of Gostynin told that he was once in Kotsk and he had a very urgent matter that he wanted to ask R. Menahem Mendel. He was wandering around the outer room that was called the small *bet midrash* but he was unable to get to the door because of the large crowd that was milling around near the door and he had great anguish over this. R. Isaac Meir of Gur saw him and asked why he did not enter, since he sensed that he needed to go in. He responded that he could see for himself that it was impossible to get near the door. While they were still talking, R. Menahem Mendel opened the door and said: Yehiel Meir Gostyininer, come in. Not only that, but he had prepared a chair for him and told him to be seated and they discussed all of his issues. [E.E. No. 13]

C.

A group of young men were sitting in Kotsk and discussing the greatness of R. Menahem Mendel. One of them said: it is impossible that the prophets should be on a higher spiritual level than what we see with our master. As soon as he finished speaking, Feivel, the *shamash,* came and said: the young man from Lodz should go in to the *Rebbe.* When he got to the door, R. Menahem Mendel called out to him in a fiery tone: So, you want to know about the spiritual level of the prophets and if our understanding is on the same level as the prophets? [E.E. No. 835]

50. Rabbinate

A.

"*Love work and hate the rabbinate*" [*m. Avot* 1.10]. This is difficult. If so, who will study for the rabbinate? However, the meaning is that you should love the work—that is the Torah, which is the work of the rabbinate, and hate the rabbinate—that is the arrogance. [E.E. No. 596]

51. Repentance

A.

R. Menahem Mendel said: Anyone who sits at my table for the third Sabbath meal and hears Torah from me, I promise him that he will not die without repenting. [S.S.K. IV:54]

[The third Sabbath meal has a long history in Hasidism and before that in Kabbalah as a time of special spiritual grace.]

B.

"One hour of repentance and good works in this world are better than the whole life in the world to come" [*m. Avot* 4:17]. R. Menahem Mendel said: this is the hour that we sit at the third meal on the Sabbath. [L.A. 130, n. 5]

C.

In *Avot* it says: "*One hour of repentance and good deeds in this world is better than the whole life in the world to come*" [*m. Avot* 4.17]. What is this hour? The intention is the time of the third Sabbath meal, after the afternoon prayer, when it is forbidden to have regular sermons or study sessions. That hour is better for repentance and reflection on his deeds in this world, on his actions and intentions. [E.E. No. 9]

D.

"*Listen you who are deaf; you blind ones, look up and see*" [Isa 42:18]. R. Menahem Mendel said: How is it possible to say to a deaf person that he should hear and to a blind person that he should see? He said: the prophet shouted that you should not be deaf and should not be blind, since it is in your hands not to be deaf or blind. [N.H. 148; S.S.K. IV:111–12; E.E. No. 66]

E.

"*Their blood was shed like water around Jerusalem, with none to bury them*" [Ps 79:3]. R. Menahem Mendel said: it sometimes happens that a person pours out his heart like water and is very regretful that he transgressed the will of the Holy One. "*Their blood was shed like water around Jerusalem*" refers to the heart. However, the important thing is to dig, from now and in the future. This is the meaning of "*with none to bury them,*" from now and in the future. [N.H. 155]

F.

R. Menahem Mendel said: R. Simhah Bunem of Przysucha said that whoever touched his door handle would not die without repenting. I say, that whoever does not repent, it will be dark for him, both in this world and in the next. [E.E. No. 324]

G.

R. Menahem Mendel was once traveling with R. Simhah Bunem. They saw a group of peasants cutting wheat. R. Simhah Bunem called one of them and showed that he was wearing shrouds under his coat and he was from the world of illusion. He returned him to his grave. Once R. Menahem Mendel was traveling with R. Hirsch Tomaszower and when they came to a bridge, they saw some peasants throwing rocks. R. Menahem Mendel said: go over to one of them and show that they are wearing shrouds under their outer garments and they are from the world of illusion. R. Hirsch said; perhaps we are also from the world of illusion. R. Menahem Mendel said: if a person has even one thought of repentance, he is certainly not one of them. [E.E. No. 331]

H.

"Rabbi [Judah the Prince] said: Yom Kippur atones for all sins in the Torah whether he repented or not" [b. Yoma 85b]. The Holy One forgives him even if he did not repent so that if the person will want to return to God after Yom Kippur, it will be easy for him to return because the Holy has removed his filthy garments, his sins and transgressions. If he had not been forgiven, it would have been very hard for him to return since he would still have all the sins from the previous year and "one sin leads to another sin" [m. Avot 4.2]. [E.E. No. 426]

I.

"Open for me an opening of repentance no bigger than the eye of a needle and I will widen it to openings through which wagons and carriages can pass through" [Song Rab. 5.2]. God desires from the person an opening and awakening, even a tiny one. However, it must be truthful, from his inner feelings and the depths of his heart, without any reservations or barriers, like the eye of the needle. Even though the hole is very small, yet it is open from end to end. [E.E. No. 531]

J.

R. Menahem Mendel said: I would be amazed if there is anyone in this generation who can truly repent, since a person needs to reach beyond the world, because *"repentance precedes the world"* [*Midrash Shohar Tov,* Ps 90:3]. [E.E. No. 624]

52. Shavuot

A.

He said. Why does it say *"the time of giving of the Torah"* and not the receiving of the Torah? There was one time of giving of the Torah, but the receiving of the Torah is every time. Also, the giving of the Torah was for everyone, but the receiving was not equal. Each one received it according to their understanding. [L.A. 130 n. 3; O.T. 65; S.S.K. I:60; E.E. No. 448]

B.

R. Menahem Mendel said. Why is the festival called *"the time of giving of the Torah"* and not the time of receiving the Torah? The reason is that the giving of the Torah was then, but the receiving of the Torah is whenever a person studies Torah. [L.T. 427, n. 30]

53. Silence

A.

It is written concerning the inhabitants of Nineveh, *"they should cry mightily to God"* [Jonah 3:8]. R. Menahem Mendel said: "this is a peasant-like form of worship." There are two kinds of silence. The first is when one cannot do anything except cry out and this is the first form of faith. Therefore, it is also written before the redemption, *"and the people were convinced"* [Exod 4:31]. However, when they were worthy to attain the level of speech and voice, there needs to be afterwards faith and silence. Therefore, when someone achieves through wisdom something that is impossible to express, silence and shame descend on him and he is silent and believes in God. That is why it later says, *"and they believed in God"* [Exod 4:31]. It is certain that crying out was not the essence, but to attain the higher category, which is silence. [E.E. No. 888]

54. Simhat Torah

A.

Why do we call *Simhat Torah*, the time of our rejoicing? This is because we make a big banquet to celebrate the completion of the Torah and everyone rejoices in it. If so, the evil inclination could drive a person into depression and despair with its machinations, heaven forbid, by saying, why are you rejoicing? Have you finished the study of the whole Torah? Therefore, it is called a time of rejoicing, to show that every person can rejoice then, because it is a time of rejoicing. [E.E. No. 523]

B.

Once on the eve of *Simhat Torah*, R. Menahem Mendel opened the door of his private room near the *bet midrash* and asked the people seated there. What is the joy in the banquet that we make for the completion of the Torah? They did not respond, so he answered himself. The joy is that we have finished the Torah and yet have not started anything, and from knowing this comes the joy. [E.E. No. 524]

55. Sin

A.

"*In all your ways acknowledge Him*" [Prov 3:6], even regarding a sin. From the power of knowing God, and with this enthusiasm, he will separate himself from a sinful act. As the verse says, "*Because he is devoted to Me I will deliver him . . . for he knows My name*" [Ps 91:14]. [S.S.K. II:86]

B.

"*Sleeping in the morning, wine at midday, and the talk of children, etc.*" R. Menahem Mendel said: "*sleeping in the morning*"—he sleeps away his younger years. "*Wine at midday*"—a plain drink of whiskey. "*Talk of children*"—that which young men spoil. "*All of these drive a person from the world*" [*m. Avot* 3:14]. [S.S.K. V:40; E.E. No. 639]

C.

"You will see only a portion of them; you will not see all of them" [Num 23:13]. R. Menahem Mendel said: *"You will see only a portion of them"*—in the individual you will be able to find a blemish [sin]. *"You will not see all of them"*—in the community of Israel as a whole, you will not find a blemish [sin]. [L.H. 56]

D.

"What do we gain by killing our brother and covering up his blood" [Gen 37:26]? If we have to cover up his blood then that is a sign that something is not right. [E.E. No. 858]

E.

R. Menahem Mendel once said to the young men. I want that you should not sin, not only because it is forbidden, but also because you will not have the free time for this. [E.E. No. 363]

F.

A Hasid told R. Menahem Mendel that he had a difficult case in court. R. Menahem Mendel responded: you will be acquitted and innocent; just see to it that you will be free of sin. [E.E. No. 655]

G.

In parshat *Vayera*, *"he was sitting at the entrance of the tent"* [Gen 18:1]. Rashi comments: to see if someone was passing by and he would invite them to his house. That is, Abraham was sitting at the entrance of his tent to see if a passerby was committing a sin, heaven forbid. He would immediately help him do penance for the sin that he had committed and afterwards would invite him into his house. [E.E. No. 229]

H.

"Do not be afraid, etc., . . . so that His fear should be on your faces so that you do not sin" [Exod 20:17]. He said to them. The fear is not that they might

die, since this is not fear of God. Rather, his fear should be specifically not to sin. [E.E. No. 389]

56. Study of Philosophy

A.

R. Menahem Mendel saw that someone was reading a book and he asked him what book was it? He responded: It is Maimonides' *Guide for the Perplexed*. R. Menahem Mendel said: to someone who has filled his belly with Talmud and commentaries, it is a *Guide*. To someone who hasn't, it is *Perplexed*. [E.E. No. 819]

57. Study of Torah

A.

In tractate *Berakhot* it says, "If a person sees troubles come upon him, let him examine his deeds, etc." [*b. Ber.* 5a]. If he examined and did not find, he should consider the neglect of Torah study, since turning away from the Torah blinds his eyes from seeing the evil that is hidden within him. If he had studied Torah appropriately, he would have seen his situation and his defects. [E.E. No. 72]

B.

"Accustom us to your Torah."[20] It is not good to perform "*commandments of men learned by rote*" [Isa 29:13]. Thus, for commandments alone, it is not good. However, to study Torah, it is good to become accustomed. [E.E. No. 586]

C.

"Whoever fulfills the Torah from poverty will in the end fulfill it from wealth" [*m. Avot* 4.9]. If you will say that he has no enjoyment from his study, in the end he will have enjoyment. From poverty is without enjoyment, and from wealth, is with enjoyment. [E.E. No. 606]

---

20. From the morning prayers.

D.

If there are people who are great scholars, they help those who are great in worship. They help each other, and if, heaven forbid, one of them is missing then the other one will also be missing. [E.E. No. 197]

E.

My great uncle, Heschel of Zawichost, asked the author of the *Sefat Emet*: if a Jew gets depressed, how should he save himself? He responded: with prayer. My uncle said that the Rabbi of Kotsk said, with Torah. The author of the *Sefat Emet* said to him: we want that He should open our hearts with His Torah and place his love and awe into our hearts. Torah is the key through which we come to love and awe and this is prayer. [E.E. No. 621]

F.

He once said in public. They associate with despicable things and they pat their bellies with a few pages of Talmud. [E.E. No. 717]

G.

A young man used to occupy himself with the practice of Hasidism and Torah study. Later, when he was busy with children and business, he did not have so much free time for Torah study and Hasidism and he apologized for this to R. Menahem Mendel. R. Menahem Mendel responded: "God wanted to benefit Israel; therefore He increased Torah and commandments for them" [*b. Mak.* 23b]. If God had given us less, we would have been able to fulfill more. When He gave us more, it became difficult to fulfill them because of the preoccupation with business. However, the Holy One extended the Torah to all things. That is, when one builds a house there is the commandment of the parapet, *mezuzah*, *sukkah*, etc. Similarly, in business, there are ethics, true measures, and theft, not looking at women, etc. this is the meaning of "*magnify and glorify the Torah*" [Isa 42:21]. [E.E. No. 741]

H.

"*Studying a passage a hundred times is not the same as studying it a hundred and one times*" [*b. Hag.* 9b]. What is the benefit if he will study it one more time? R. Menahem Mendel said: if he studies it a hundred times and he takes the One, that is God, to help him, then there will be a great benefit. [E.E. No. 780]

I.

R. Menahem Mendel once asked R. Hirsch Tomaszower. How is it that the whole Oral Torah is fulfilled through a sin? The whole Oral Torah was not supposed to have been written down, and was only written down because of "*a time to act*"[21] [*b. Tem.* 14b]. He answered his own question. He believed that only hints and allusions were written down and this is not forbidden. [E.E. No. 849]

J.

The rabbi of Sochaczew said in the name of R. Menahem Mendel that the study of a page of Talmud purifies like a *mikvah*. [E.E. No. 853]

K.

My father [Abraham of Sochaczew], said in the name of my grandfather [the *Rebbe* of Kotsk], the study of the [Talmudic] Order of Holy Things [*Kodeshim*] purifies one's thoughts. [L.A. 134, n. 3; E.E. No. 44]

L.

He said to a merchant. Every day you should steal an hour for yourself in order to reflect on why you came into the world and how you spend your time, and study Talmud at least an hour a day. Concerning what the Talmudic sages say: "*One who sets aside time for the study of Torah violates the Torah.*" [*Midrash Shmuel* 1:1] However, this only applies to someone who has time to study all day, but a busy merchant is obligated to steal one hour. [L.H. 5; S.S.K. IV:112; E.E. No. 127]

M.

"*Train a lad in the way he ought to go; he will not swerve from it even in old age*" [Prov 22:6]. He said: Scripture warns us that the old person should

21. Ps 119:126.

not swerve from educating himself. [R.Z., *Elijah Zuta*, ch. 14, 39 n. 8; E.E. No. 138]

N.

R. Menahem Mendel said: if one does not study Torah, he will not know how to examine his sins. [S.S.K. V:44]

O.

A young man came to Kotsk and R. Menahem Mendel asked about his studies. He responded that he had studied the whole Talmud. R. Menahem Mendel responded: and what did the Talmud teach you? [S.S.K. I:72]

P.

Someone once said to the Kotsker that he wanted his children to study Torah. He responded: if you truly want them to study Torah, then you should study and they will see you studying and they will learn from it. If not, then your children will also not study, but they too will tell their children to study. [S.S.K. V:46; E.E. No. 649]

Q.

R. Menahem Mendel told his son-in-law, R. Abraham of Sochaczew. The Baal Shem Tov came into this world and brought a new path in the worship of the Lord, through Hasidism. This was not because this path was more elevated than the path of Torah study that had been practiced previously. Rather, because of our many sins, the Torah was damaged by the many false casuistic interpretations [*pilpulim*] that were offered by rabbis, like the one that Pharaoh reasoned like the Talmudic sages Abbaye and Ravah. There was great distress in Heaven and there was no other solution, but to send the holy Baal Shem Tov to this world to inaugurate a new path. Aside from this, the path of Torah study is more elevated and is still the preferred path to come closer to the Holy One. [A.R. no. 110]

R.

"The teachings of the Lord is his delight, and with his Torah, etc." [Ps 1:2]. Rashi explains that it is first called the Torah of the Lord. That is, the Torah that will come to him through work, struggle and effort will be a permanent acquisition, and he will completely cleave to it until the Torah itself will teach him all of its paths. However, if he will not exert himself, then nothing will remain with him. [E.E. No. 876]

S.

I once was visiting R. Menahem Mendel of Kotsk and I asked him, what should I do to have greater desire to study? He was very surprised. How is it possible not to desire something so good? Then he told me to study with greater devotion. [E.E. No. 913]

T.

"You must help him lift it" [Deut 22:4]. Help comes to a person to help him with Torah study and worship, only if the person exerts himself. Only then, is he helped. [E.E. No. 510]

U.

Moses Yeruhem, the son of R. Menahem Mendel, studied with the Rabbi of Brock. Once, during his period of seclusion, the Rabbi of Brock entered his private room with Moses Yeruhem so that R. Menahem Mendel should hear the lesson that they had studied in tractate b. *Ketubot* 9b: *"Everyone who went to war with the house of David wrote his wife a bill of divorce."* At that time, a Hasid was sitting in the *bet midrash* for a long time and was not able to enter in order to take his leave. When he heard a conversation inside the room, he opened the door and stuck his head in. R. Menahem Mendel said: what do you want? He responded that he wanted to depart. R. Menahem Mendel responded: have you heard what we have been discussing here? The one who went to war with the house of David wrote his wife a bill of divorce. You have a *bet midrash*. Go there and return to your studies. [E.E. No. 366]

[It was customary that a Hasid would greet the *Rebbe* when he came for a visit and also say goodbye before leaving at the end of his visit. The Hasid could not leave without formally saying goodbye to the *Rebbe*.]

V.

R. Menahem Mendel once called Feivel, *his shamash*, and said to him. Feivel, what do you think is the meaning of the phrase, "the Torah was only given to be interpreted by eaters of manna." [*Mek. Beshallah* 17] He responded: I think it means whoever does not lack income, like the eaters of manna. R. Menahem Mendel said to him: ignoramus, and what about "*And Jeshurun grew fat and kicked*" [Deut 32:15]. I think the intention is for Jews who only have enough income for the day and don't worry about tomorrow. [E.E. No. 625]

58. Torah

A.

The Rabbi of Gostynin said in the name of R. Menahem Mendel. Every author makes an introduction for his book. It is a popular saying that a book without an introduction is like a body without a soul. Therefore, the Holy One also made an introduction for His book and it is good manners (*derekh eretz*), since "good manners (*derekh eretz*) precedes Torah" [*Lev. Rab.* 9.3]. [E.E. No. 449]

B.

"Good manners (*derekh eretz*) precedes Torah" [*Lev. Rab.* 9.3]. He said: *Derekh eretz* is the introduction to Torah. Just as a person can know the character of a book from its introduction, in the same way, *derekh eretz* is the introduction to Torah. The character of a person's Torah [teachings] can be discerned from his behavior. [O.T., 7; S.S.K. I:66; E.E. No. 297]

C.

"*See, I set before you*" [Deut 11:26]. The verse begins in the singular and ends in the plural. R. Menahem Mendel said that the Torah was given to all of Israel, but not everyone sees it equally. [L.H. 62]

D.

"*We will do and we will hear*" [Exod 24: 7] is written in the plural, but everyone spoke for themselves. It should have been "*I will do and I will hear.*" However, because of the pleasantness and sweetness of the Torah which was so beloved by them that each one became a guarantor for his friend. [S.S.K. I:90]

E.

From a person who conducts himself according to the Torah, one can learn how to be a true Jew. [E.E. No. 190]

F.

"*For your love is more delightful than wine*" [Song 1:2]. The Midrash [*Song Rab.* 1.2] said: more than the wine of Torah. He said: There are many forms of *devekut* [communion] through which one can cleave to the Holy One. The form of *devekut* that is most appropriate is through the Torah. [L.T. 424, n. 3; S.S.K. III:25; A.R. no. 110; E.E. No. 33]

G.

A Kotsker Hasid was arguing with a Hasid of another group. The Kotsker Hasid said: your *Rebbe* teaches Torah to the Heavens, but our *Rebbe* teaches Torah to the *pupik*. [S.S.K. IV:21]

H.

A Kotsker Hasid was visiting the court of another *zaddiq* and listened to his teachings. They were very exalted and wondrous. The Kotsker Hasid was asked his opinion about the teachings. He responded: they are indeed wondrous teachings that touched all the limbs, but he did not talk about the *pupik*, and in Kotsk, the *pupik* is the most important thing. [S.S.K. V:44]

I.

"*Buy Truth and never sell it*" [Prov 23:23]. R. Menahem Mendel asked a question. If the verse warns the one who has Truth not to sell it, where can it be found to be purchased? He answered: Truth, this is the Torah, and you purchase it through exertion. If you exerted yourself and have found it, do not sell it for your benefit. [L.H. 77; E.E. No. 575].

J.

"Ben Bag-Bag said: Turn it and turn it again for everything is in it. Contemplate it and grow gray and old over it and do not move away from it since you cannot have a better rule" [*m. Avot* 5.22]. The meaning of "do not move away from it" is, do not move away from the Torah. You cannot have a better rule, because there is no better rule than the Torah. [E.E. No. 608]

K.

R. Isaac Meir of Gur said to the Rabbi of Aleksandrow. Just as there was thunder and lightning when the Torah was received at Sinai, there is thunder and lightning now when the Torah is being received in Tomaszow. [E.E. No. 379]

L.

When the rabbi of Gostynin came home after *Shavuot* from Kotsk, his father-in-law asked him if they had received the Torah any differently there. He responded, certainly. How? The rabbi said: How do you interpret, "do not steal"? His father-in-law responded, do not steal from others. He responded: the Rabbi of Kotsk explains it: one should not steal from oneself. [E.E. No. 497]

[This comment is also attributed to the R. Simhah Bunem of Przysucha in other sources.]

M.

There is an evil impulse, heaven forbid, that attracts the person to a distorted understanding of the Torah and one needs to guard against it. [E.E. No. 500]

N.

"Our forefathers in Egypt did not perceive Your wonders, etc." [Ps106:7] . . .
"They believed His words and sang His praises" [Ps 106:12]. The miracle
brings amazement to the person temporarily and then it is forgotten. However, through the Torah, faith is strengthened and made permanent. That
is why it is written that our forefathers did not come to an understanding
of the faith through miracles, but they believed His words and sang His
praises. [E.E. No. 563]

59. Truth

A.

R. Menahem Mendel once asked R. Isaac Meir of Gur about the verse,
"truth springs from the earth" [Ps 85:12]. What does one plant in the earth
that truth should sprout from it? Isaac Meir answered him, if you bury
falsehood, then the truth will sprout from the earth. [S.S.K. IV:102; E.E.
No. 121]

B.

Rabbi Zelig of Shrensk traveled to Kotsk several times and said *"Truth
sprouts from the earth"* [Ps 85:12]. The *gematria* of *"earth"* is "Kotsk."[22]
[E.E. No. 15]

C.

R. Abraham of Sochaczew once said. In the days of the Holy Yehudi [of
Przysucha] they began to teach the path of truth. In Kotsk, they taught
more and more on the edge. They said, this is false and that is false and
clarified the path of truth even more. [S.S.K. IV:94–95]

D.

R. Menahem Mendel asked. What was the sin of the spies? [Numbers 13]
They told the truth that they had seen giants and people being buried.[23]

22. The numerical value of both words is 291.
23. An allusion to Num 13:32, *"a land that devours its settlers."*

The truth does not mean that they would say about a fact that it is so, since if they say otherwise, that would be a lie. They are not liars, but would be called, men of truth. Rather, it is so. If the person imagines that the matter appears to be contrary to the word of God, and he exerts himself and uses all sorts of strategies to find the true word of God, this is the intention of truth. This was the sin of the spies that they did not want to delve into the matter, to find the true word of God, like Joshua and Caleb. [N.H. 100; E.E. No. 462]

E.

God's seal is truth, because the seal must be something that cannot be forged. Truth cannot be forged, since if it is forged, it is no longer truth. [O.T. 79; E.E. No. 481]

F.

"*Speak the truth from his heart*" [Ps15:2]. He should accustom the truth to dwell in his heart. [E.E. No. 159]

G.

Rabbi Isaac Meir of Gur said that he saw that it was still possible to acquire truth in Tomaszow. [E.E. No. 268]

H.

"*And God said, let us make man in our image, after our likeness, etc.*" [Gen 1:26]. It says in Midrash Rabbah [*Gen. Rab.* 8.5]: "R. Simon said: When the Holy One wanted to created man, the ministering angels divided into two groups. Some said that he should be created and some said that he should not be created, as it is written, "*Lovingkindness and truth meet; justice and well-being kiss*" [Ps 85:11]. Lovingkindness said that he should be created, because he will do deeds of lovingkindness. Truth said that he should not be created, because he is full of falsehoods. Justice said that he should be created, because he will do just deeds. Peace said that he should not be created, because he is full of conflict. What did the Holy One do? He took truth and flung it to the earth, as it says, "*He hurled truth to the ground*" [Dan 8:12]."

The words of the Midrash do not appear to be understandable. Even if He hurled Truth to the ground, Peace is still standing and arguing that man should not be created, because he is full of conflict. What is the response to this argument? One would say that this argument for the sake of Heaven grows out of the enthusiasm of clarifying and understanding that Truth is the correct and proper path in the worship of God. One said that it is the true and correct path and the other one said differently. However, if one throws away the Truth then there will be Peace. By throwing Truth to the ground, the Holy One made peace among the ministering angels and they all agreed that man should be created, by means of the disappearance of Truth. [O.T. p. 5–6]

I.

"*And He hurled truth to the earth*" [Dan 8:12]. The Holy One took the truth and hurled it to the earth. It is not understandable why He hurled truth, since peace also argued that man should not be created, since he is full of strife. However, the matter is thus. When there is an argument for the sake of heaven, and one says that this is the truth and someone says something else, if one throws away the truth then there will certainly be peace. [E.E. No. 294]

J.

Concerning the same matter. It would seem that truth and peace opposed justice and lovingkindness. Why didn't the Holy One hurl peace to the earth and leave only truth in opposition to justice and lovingkindness? Menahem Mendel said: the majority could not be only opposed to the pleas of peace. However, against the truth that argues that he should not be created because he is full of falsehoods, the pleas of justice and lovingkindness could not prevail. [E.E. No. 295]

60. Unity

A.

R. Menahem Mendel said that he only looked at the good points that every Jew has, since if he does not connect himself with all the children of Israel, then falsehood will rule him. The letters of the word falsehood [*SheKeR*] are a permutation of the word connection [*KeSheR*]. We find in the generation of Saul that they were defeated in battle because they were not united, while in the generation of Ahab, they were victorious because they were united. [S.S.K. IV:109–110]

B.

Haman's accusation against Israel was that they were dispersed and had no unity. Therefore, Esther said to Mordecai: "*go and assemble them*" [Esth 4:16]. That is, they should become united. [E.E. No. 529]

61. Worship

A.

"*The earth is full of your creations*" [Ps 104:24]. A person can learn how to serve the Lord from every thing. [S.S.K. I:68]

B.

He said concerning the verse, "*Do not worship the Lord in like manner*" [Deut 12:4]. For the Lord one does not do things this way. This means that one should not perform the commandments in a haphazard manner, "*a commandment of men, learned by rote*" [Isa 29:13]. Rather, there should be preparation before the performance [of the commandments]. [S.S.K. I:71; E.E. 503]

C.

He said, concerning the verse, "*You shall serve the Lord your God and He will bless your bread and your water*" [Exod 23:25]. The first part of the verse is in the plural and the second part is singular. This is because all sacred acts need to be done in the community of Israel and in the name of all Israel. Therefore, divine service is in the plural. However, physical things, even eating, are individual. Each person's food enters his body and does not affect the body of his friend. We find that the study of Torah and prayer, even when done alone, are done together with the whole community of Israel. But physical things, even when done in a group, are done individually. I heard this from him in a private meeting. [R.Z., *Elijah Zuta*, II, ch. 14, 38, n. 3; L.H., 39; O.T. 41; E.E. No. 56]

D.

"*The Lord exits forever, your words stand firm in Heaven*" [Ps 119:89]. How long will you stand at a distance while the Holy One desires your worship? [R.Z., *Elijah Rabah*, I, ch. 6, 106]

E.

R. Simhah Bunem asked R. Menahem Mendel. From where did he derive his awakening to worship the Lord? He responded: from this verse, "*lift up your eyes and see: who created these?*" [Isa 40:26]. R. Simhah Bunem said: Every person can attain awakening from this. The awakening of a Jew should be from the exodus from Egypt. [L.T. 424, n. 1; E.E. No. 34]

F.

"*And the Philistines stopped up all the wells which his father's servants had dug in the days of his father Abraham, filling them with earth*" [Gen 26:15]. "*Isaac dug anew the wells that had been dug in the days of his father Abraham, etc.*" [Gen 26:18]. This means that the Philistines began to follow the practices and attributes of Abraham our Father. They began to imitate, and this is the meaning of "*filling them with earth,*" as Abraham said, "*I am but dust and ashes*" [Gen 18:27], and because of this, the wells were filled up. Isaac returned and began to dig another well and to follow another custom and attribute in his worship of the Lord. [S.S.K. II:17; E.E. No. 156]

G.

"*With all your heart*" [Deut 6:5]. "*With both your inclinations*" [*m. Ber.* 9.5]. If he does not have an evil inclination then worship is very difficult. When he desires it, then the evil part also helps him, since it was created for this purpose. [S.S.K. I:61]

H.

"*See how the man hastens with his work*" [Prov 22:29]. This is seemingly difficult. A commandment needs to be done with deliberateness and not haste. It appears to me that the preparation for performing a commandment needs to be done with deliberateness, but it is better that the performance of the commandment itself needs to be done with haste. It is like the builder. If he is a master artisan, he designs the structure of the house on paper with great deliberateness, in order that later when he does the actual work he will be able to work quickly. That is why it is written with his work and not to his work. [E.E. No. 530]

I.

"You shall eat by the labor of your hands" [Ps 128:2]. It should only be by the labor of your hands and not with your heart and mind. The heart and mind need to be set aside for the worship of God. [E.E. No. 567]

J.

"A voice calls out. Clear a road in the desert for the Lord" [Isa 40:3]. This means, someone who is not beholden to anything in this world and feels himself to be free without any connection to anything, from such a person can the sound emanate spontaneously and call out, clear a path for the worship of God. [E.E. No. 839]

62. The *Zaddiq*

A.

He once said to a contemporary *zaddiq* that he was a *zaddiq* in a fur [*zaddiq* in *pelz*]. He meant that there is one who wears warm clothes in order to keep warm in the winter. There is another one who heats the whole house. What is the difference between them? One of them wears warm clothes, but this does not help others at all. However, the one who heats the house also does good for others. [N. H. 8–9; S.S.K. IV:109; E.E. No. 124]

B.

Ordinary people are able, heaven forbid, to damage the *zaddiq* with their thoughts. However, the Sages repaired this when they said, *"the fear of your teacher is like the fear of Heaven"* [*m. Avot* 4:12]. Because of the fear of their teacher, they are separated from him and stand at a distance, and they cannot harm him. [L.T. 428 n. 48]

C.

In the Midrash concerning Jethro [*Exod. Rab.* 27.2]. *"The wise will inherit honor"* [Prov 3:35]. This was Jethro when he came to Moses, they all went out to greet him. The question is, do *zaddiqim* seek honor? They run away from honor! However, the answer is that the wise offer others honor in order to test them. Moses was testing Jethro in this way. [E.E. No. 372]

D.

He once said: Do not think that if the generation is great they need a great rabbi and a minor rabbi is enough for a small generation. It is the opposite. The smaller and humbler the generation the greater a rabbi they need. It is just like a sick person. The sicker the person, the more expert a physician he needs. [S.S.K. I:89]

E.

"The Lord became angry with Moses" [Exod 14:4]. At first Moses was unwilling to go to Pharaoh. However, afterwards when God's anger that the Israelites were in bondage in Egypt also angered Moses, he went to liberate them. It should be the same with every *zaddiq*. Everything that he does for the community of Israel should be because there burns within him God's anger that the Israelites are under the domination of the Evil Side [*Sitra Achra*]. Then the *zaddiq* can do good for them. [E.E. No. 186]

F.

A *zaddiq*, one of his opponents, once sent a message to R. Menahem Mendel telling him that he was so great and his understanding was so great that it reached the seventh heaven. R. Menahem Mendel responded that he was so small that all seven heavens lower themselves for him. [S.S.K. II:26; E.E. No. 189]

G.

Why is a *Rebbe* called a "good Jew" [*guter yid*], because he has been clarified and is completely good. [L.T. 427 n. 32; A.R. No. 74; E.E. No. 240]

H.

"Moses did as the Lord commanded him and the community assembled" [Lev 8:4]. R. Isaac of Warka once visited R. Menahem Mendel, who said to him. In the future we will have to give an account for every journey that a Jew made to us. He then quoted the above-cited verse. The explanation is that when Moses did as God commanded him, then the community assembled. When the *zaddiq* does the will of God, then the hearts of Israel are drawn to him, and what are the obligations of the *zaddiq* to those who come to him? [N.H. 81; O.T. 53; E.E. No. 618]

I.

"The Lord loves zaddiqim" [Ps 146:8]. Someone asked R. Menahem Mendel, why did King David, of blessed memory, place the *zaddiq* among the disabled that they should be counted among *"restores sight to the blind, etc."*? [N.H. 159]

J.

In the Midrash [*Gen. Rab.* 39.1], there is a parable about someone who saw a citadel burning, etc., until the Holy One revealed himself and said to him, I am the owner of the citadel. When R. Menahem Mendel taught this Midrash to his disciples and said the words, "I am the owner of the citadel," a great fear descended on all those standing there and they all felt that there was an owner of the citadel. [L.H. 11–12; E.E. No. 128]

K.

R. Menahem Mendel once asked a Hasid about the customs and practices of the *zaddiq* to which he traveled. He responded that he shows miracles and wonders. Then Menahem Mendel asked him, could he cause a miracle to make someone a Hasid? [E.E. No. 174]

L.

An important rabbi who was an opponent of R. Menahem Mendel asked him: who was the true *zaddiq* in the generation, thinking that he would certainly not name himself. He responded: What if you don't know who the true *zaddiq* is, but it is a doubt for you? He is like a mote in the eye. If you knew who was the true *zaddiq*, your opposition to him would be even greater. [S.S.K. V:46; E.E. No. 648]

M.

"*Moses did as the Lord commanded him. When the community was assembled, etc.*" [Lev 8:4]. When the *zaddiq* does the will of the Holy One, he awakens the hearts of Israel to be drawn to him and to learn from his ways. [E.E. No. 414]

N.

"*Joshua ben Nun and Caleb ben Yefuneh were among those who scouted the land, etc.*" [Num 14:6]. It is known that they were among the scouts, but they were also leaders of the Israelites. They certainly wore *shtreimels* and white kaftans. Now that they spoke ill about the land of Israel, then Joshua and Caleb who were among the scouts "*tore their garments.*" Why are you still wearing *shtreimels*? [E.E. No. 495; E.E. No. 904]

O.

"*Who is Aaron that you should rail against him?*" [Num 16:11]. That is, do you know who Aaron is that you come to argue against him? [E.E. No. 499]

P.

"*The zaddiq flourishes like a palm tree*" [Ps 92:13]. It is necessary for the *zaddiq* to flourish. [E.E. No. 561]

Q.

He said concerning the controversies of the *zaddiqim* of his generation. "Every controversy that is for the sake of heaven will be fulfilled in the end" [*m. Avot* 5.17]. That is, in future generations their descendants will marry each other and they will be united. [E.E. No. 725]

R.

R. Menahem Mendel asked R. Isaac Meir of Gur. Why were Aaron and Miriam punished when they spoke about Moses, since they were right? [Numbers 12] R. Isaac Meir of Gur responded: they should have spoken to Moses first. R. Menahem Mendel said: and what if they were afraid to talk to the *Rebbe*? [E.E. No. 806]

S.

The *Rebbe's* greetings to people; saying hello to the *Rebbe* is "*ma'aseh Bereshit*" and saying goodbye to him is "*ma'aseh Merkavah*." [E.E. No. 871]

["Ma'aseh Bereshit"—the doctrine of Creation and "Ma'aseh Merkavah"—the doctrine of the Heavenly Throne are considered to be the most esoteric teachings of Rabbinic Judaism.]

T.

"*Do not curse God*" [Exod 22:27]. Do not curse a man of God. [E.E. No. 773]

63. The *Zaddiq* and his Powers

A.

He once asked a Hasid, what he did for a living. He responded that he was a bread baker. Our master said to him: your bread is assured to you all your days. So it was. He lived to be almost a hundred years old and always a plentiful income. [S.S.K. II:97; E.E. No. 215]

B.

One day a Hasid asked his advice about a proposed marriage. The *Rebbe* did not give him a clear answer and the Hasid entreated him that he should give him a clear answer. The *Rebbe* said to him: Do you really imagine that when someone comes to ask advice that we ascend to heaven and open the record book to see what is written there? And if someone else comes immediately afterwards with his question, we again open the Heavenly record book to look into it, etc. The matter is thus. When someone comes to ask advice, we come to a level of pride, but where there is pride there is no common sense. Thus, we are forced to work to quash the pride. Once we have done this, we have to see if the matter is appropriate according to the laws of the Torah. Afterwards, if it is appropriate according to justice, and then we can offer advice. It is impossible to give advice in any other manner. [S.S.K. IV:57–58; E.E. No. 114]

C.

When I [R. Samuel of Shinove] was the rabbi in Waldowa, the holy Rabbi of Kotsk, may his soul be in the Heavenly Treasury, visited and told me the following story. There was a wealthy innkeeper who lived between Kotsk and Leczna. He lived there for a number of years, had children and walked in the just path. The local nobleman wanted to raise his rent and threatened to force him out if he refused. He traveled to Leczna and the *Rebbe* there told him that he should not pay even an additional penny in rent. If he was forced out, he should go and live elsewhere. As the deadline got closer, he returned to the *Rebbe* a second and a third time, but he received no other answer. When the nobleman began to pressure him greatly, he traveled to Kotsk to me, and told me everything that happened and I told him to pay the additional rent and not to move. When he heard this, he ran to the nobleman, paid him, and remained in his place in peace. A few days later, his wife went outside and became very weak in all her senses and limbs. There was a great outcry, since she was the housekeeper and the whole family depended on her. He immediately traveled to Leczna, but the *Rebbe* would not see them in any circumstances. The *Rebbe*'s servants said that they were not responsible for this, but rather it was the responsibility of the *Rebbe* of Kotsk, because they had followed his advice. Afterwards, they came before the *Rebbe* and he said, "God will save" and God saved her and she was healed.

Perhaps there might be some contention between us? However, I will tell you the story. When the villager came to me and told me the story and also what the *Rebbe* of Leczna had told him, I understood his intention. He saw with his wisdom that it was not good for him to remain there. The Holy One advised him this way, in order to rescue the householder, and therefore he did not say more. However, I understood that this was not the best course. I understood his situation and how involved he was in his business. I believed that it was a greater danger for the householder and his children, if they would be uprooted and I chose this path. There is no contradiction to the words of the *Rebbe* of Leczna, heaven forbid. I thought this was a greater danger. [R.Z., *Elijah Zutah*, II, ch. 6, 22–24; E.E. No. 54]

D.

R. Menahem Mendel once asked his disciple Barukh Stichiner, why doesn't he ask him advice about suitable marriage partners. He responded that he had received a tradition that regarding suitable marriage partners, even the *Rebbe* has no special knowledge. R. Menahem Mendel responded: nonetheless, the *Rebbe* can at least give friendly advice. [E.E. No. 91]

E.

He did not advise people to divorce because they had no children. Once somebody pleaded with him greatly. He responded: if you want children who will be completely evil, tell me. The person changed the subject. [E.E. No. 146]

F.

Once the Rabbis of Gostynin and Strykow were in Kotsk. They looked through the keyhole to see what R. Menahem Mendel was doing. R. Menahem Mendel felt this and went to the door. The Rabbi of Strykow immediately ran away, but the Rabbi of Gostynin was not able to run away and concealed himself. R. Menahem Mendel asked him, who was the second one, and he was required to answer. R. Menahem Mendel commanded that he be called and he said to them I have one question of you, and they stood in fear. Two petitions were brought to me. One was from a dying person, heaven forbid, and the other from a woman in difficult childbirth. One was waiting on the other. They didn't respond from great fear and he said to them. I want that you should give me an answer. The Rabbi of Strykow answered, if such a matter came before me, I would be forced to intercede with God to send a new soul to the woman in difficult childbirth and the other would remain alive. He was amazed at this and said: you have answered well, and so it was. [E.E. No. 746]

G.

Once R. Menahem Mendel was ill and he sent a messenger with a *kvitel* to R. Baer of Radoshitz. He ordered the messenger not to reveal who the sick person was that sent the *kvitel*. The messenger handed over the *kvitel* to the *Rebbe* that the sick person should be blessed. However, after a few seconds of thought the *Rebbe* called out, this is the *Rebbe* of Kotsk. When the messenger heard these words, he was afraid that the *Rebbe* would regret the blessing for a complete recovery that he has just blessed the owner of the *kvitel*, since there was a controversy at that time between the followers of Kotsk and those of Radoshitz. He asked: will the *Rebbe* of Kotsk not be blessed with a complete recovery? The *Rebbe* responded: listen my son and I will educate you. The *Rebbe* of Kotsk and I disagree in this matter. The worship and spiritual path of the *Rebbe* of Kotsk is in the category of *"subordinate your will to His will"* [*m. Avot* 2.4], but my theory is *"The Holy One decrees and the zaddiq abrogates"* [*b. Moed Kat.* 16b]. That is why he sent it to me anonymously. However, I have already blessed him with a full recovery. [E.E. No. 836]

H.

Hasidim sent *kvitlach* to R. Menahem Mendel with the Rabbi of Gostynin. The Rabbi of Gostynin prayed for these people during the whole journey. When he came to R. Menahem Mendel, he placed the *kvitlach* on the table. R. Menahem Mendel said to him: why did you bring me *kvitlach* whose pleas have already been answered. [E.E. No. 177]

I.

Once R. Menahem Mendel and the Rabbi of Radzymin were traveling to Przysucha. They reached about two kilometers from Przysucha on a Friday and it got dark and they had to spend the Sabbath in a village where there no Jews lived. Since they did not have any lights for the Sabbath, the Rabbi of Radzymin said that it would be necessary to use the light from the six days of creation for illumination. So it was and the house was filled with light. After the third Sabbath meal, R. Menahem Mendel said that they had used the light enough and the light immediately disappeared and it became dark. [E.E. No. 93]

J.

The rabbi of Pilica, Phinehas Elijah, once said in a humorous manner to his uncle, R. Isaac Meir of Gur that Hasidim told about R. Menahem Mendel that when he rattled the doorknob, all the seven heavens shook. R. Isaac Meir responded that it was true. Whoever did not believe that when the *Rebbe* shook his hat, all the heavens shook, would not be able to receive anything good from him. [E.E. No. 637]

K.

There was a famous scribe in Kotsk who wrote a Torah scroll for R. Menahem Mendel, and R. Menahem Mendel did not allow him to complete it. R. Israel Meir of Gostynin knew the scribe and asked R. Menahem Mendel about this. He responded that the scribe had an inappropriate thought and therefore he was concerned that the scroll was not correct. [E.E. No. 681]

L.

R. Menahem Mendel felt during the Torah reading that there occurred to the reader an incorrect explanation of a verse that he was reading and he ordered him to stop. Later, he was allowed to complete the reading. [E.E. No. 682]

64. Miscellaneous Teachings

A.

We eat fish on the Sabbath because other living things [that we eat] have the commandments of slaughtering and salting. However, fish have no specific commandment, so we create for them the commandment of eating them on the Sabbath. [E.E. No. 22]

B.

Once something was stolen from R. Menahem Mendel's house. Feivel, the *shamash* said that it is no wonder. Everything here was a free for all, so why shouldn't someone steal. R. Menahem Mendel shouted at him. It is written

in the Torah, "*do not steal*" [Exod 20:13]. The prohibition is like a big wall.
[E.E. No. 820]

C.

It is not appropriate to say everything we think, nor is it appropriate to
write down everything we say, nor print everything we write. [E.E. No. 989]

D.

"*The whole people saw the sounds*" [Exod 20:15]. The people saw and
looked at the externalities of the matter, like thunder and lightning, etc.
[E.E. No. 611]

E.

"*In the end you will listen*" [Deut 7:12]. In the end you will be forced to
listen; if so, it is better that you listen immediately. [E.E. No. 208]

F.

He said: If one of the sides in a rabbinic trial [*din Torah*] cries, this is also in
the category of bribery. [E.E. No. 176]

G.

R. Menahem Mendel once had a very beautiful *etrog* and he showed it to all
of his disciples and they all praised the *etrog*. He showed to R. Ze'ev Wolf of
Strykow, who said that it was not good. He understood that if R. Menahem
Mendel had asked all of them, it was a sign that there was something wrong
and therefore he agreed with his teacher. [E.E. No. 87]

H.

He was once speaking with a disciple, dressed in shirtsleeves and a *kippah*
on his head. The disciple asked about R. Isaac Meir of Gur. He immediately
went to his room for a few minutes and returned dressed in his jacket, *gartel*
and his *spodek* on his head. He said; it is not respectful to speak of him
when not formally attired. [E.E. No. 265]

I.

R. Isaac Meir of Gur once took his two grandsons to Kotsk during a particularly cold period. Someone asked him if they lacked so much Hasidic teachings during this period? He responded with a smile. The difficult journey was worth it so that they should see a true Jew. [E.E. No. 266]

J.

Shifting a person's home from one city to another is a very great matter. If he was asked about that, it was a very difficult question for him. It is a matter of shifting the root of his soul, since the place of a person below, has its root above [in Heaven]. [E.E. No. 231]

K.

In parshat *Vayigash*, "*Jacob blessed Pharaoh*" [Gen 47:7]. If Pharaoh received from Jacob, it would be impossible for him [Pharaoh] to have dominion over him [Jacob]. [E.E. No. 232]

L.

The Ten Statements were revealed to Israel through the ten plagues that were brought on the Egyptians. Every plague was one Statement. From the plague of darkness, the statement of "*And there was light*" [Gen 1:3] was revealed to Israel. [E.E. 233]

M.

It is written in Midrash *Tanh. Phinehas* [10]: "Just like their faces are not identical, their ideas are not identical." Just as you are able to tolerate the face of a person whose face is not identical to yours, so to you should be able to tolerate someone's ideas that are not identical to yours. [E.E. No. 629]

N.

In his latter years, R. Menahem Mendel had great pains in his eyes on a number of occasions. A physician advised him to wear glasses during study. However, R. Menahem Mendel did not want to wear the glasses during study because he did not want to place a barrier between his eyes and the holy Torah. [E.E. No. 783]

[The same story is told about a number of Hasidic masters. It is a standard trope in Hasidic hagiography.]

Appendix I: The Kotsk Song

[The source of this song is unknown.]

To Kotsk, one does not travel in a vehicle.

To Kotsk, one goes on foot.

Since Kotsk is in place of the Temple,

Since Kotsk is in place of the Temple.

To Kotsk one needs to make a pilgrimage (*oleh regel*),

Make a pilgrimage.

Since the translation of *regel* is a foot,

To Kotsk one needs to go on foot, singing and dancing.

When Hasidim go to Kotsk, they go with song, and when Hasidim go to Kotsk, they go with song.

To Kotsk, one does not travel in a vehicle.

To Kotsk, one goes on foot.

Since Kotsk is in place of the Temple,

Since Kotsk is in place of the Temple.

To Kotsk one needs to make a pilgrimage (*oleh regel*),

Make a pilgrimage.

Since the translation of *regel* is a habit.

One needs to habituate oneself to go to Kotsk, singing and dancing.

When Hasidim go to Kotsk, they go with a dance, and when Hasidim go to Kotsk, they go with a dance.

To Kotsk, one does not travel in a vehicle.

To Kotsk, one goes on foot.

Since Kotsk is in place of the Temple,

Since Kotsk is in place of the Temple.

To Kotsk one needs to make a pilgrimage (*oleh regel*),

Make a pilgrimage.

Since the translation of *regel* is a holiday.

Good Yom Tov, Good Yom Tov, Good Yom Tov, Good Yom Tov.

When Hasidim go to Kotsk, it is a great holiday, and when Hasidim go to Kotsk, it is a great holiday.

Appendix II: The Friday Night Incident

The Friday Night Incident in Kotsk: History of a Legend[1]

THE ANTINOMIAN LEGEND OF the "Friday Night Incident" in Kotsk is one of the best-known Hasidic tales. Its truth or falsehood has been discussed for the last seventy years. In essence, it reports that on a Friday night in the winter of 1839, R. Menahem Mendel of Kotsk, at a gathering of his followers, either touched the candlesticks or extinguished the candles, thereby desecrating the Sabbath. While doing this he is alleged to have muttered, "There is no Law, and there is no Judge."[2] In other words, there is no God. Shortly thereafter, R. Menahem Mendel either locked himself or was locked into his study, where he remained until his death, approximately twenty years later. This essay presents an overview of the legend's literary history and an analysis of its truth or falsity.

The first published reference to R. Menahem Mendel's supposed heresy appears in an 1896 novella by A. N. Frenk entitled *Me-Hayyei ha-Hasidim be-Polin*.[3] In a passing reference to R. Menahem Mendel of Kotsk, one of the main characters tells his companion that he was present when the Friday night incident occurred. He recounts how at one Friday night gathering (*tish*) R. Menahem Mendel appeared to be very nervous and agitated. His eyes glowed like torches and he kept fidgeting in his seat. Suddenly he got up and called out,

> "My sons, do what your heart desires, for there is no Law and there is no Judge!" The gathering was astounded. Menahem Mendel

---

1. An earlier version of this appendix was published in, Faierstein, *All Is in the Hand of Heaven*, 1989, 2005.

2. "*Let din ve-let Dayan.*" See, *Targum Jonathan* to Gen 4:8.

3. Frenk came from a Hasidic background but became a *maskil*. Like many of his contemporaries with similar backgrounds, his attitudes toward Hasidism were negative. He is not a reliable witness. On Frenk see, *Encyclopedia Judaica*, 7:159.

continued, "You don't believe me? Here is a sign: it is the Sabbath. See what I do!" With these words he grabbed the lit candle.[4]

Frenk's account does not appear to have made much of an impression or created any controversy. He is not mentioned by any later authors until the recent work by A. J. Heschel.[5]

In 1904, S. Y. Yutzkin, in an article entitled "Pereq mi-Toldot ha-Hasidut be-Polonia," briefly discusses R. Menahem Mendel of Kotsk and mentions some rumors concerning him. Certain of Yutzkin's statements[6] indicate that he has confused Kotsk with Ruzhin-Sadogora and R. Menahem Mendel with R. Dov Baer of Leova, the son of R. Israel of Ruzhin, who flirted with *Haskalah*.[7]

In 1918, R. J. L. Slotnick, published an article in *Reshumot*[8] on R. Menahem Mendel of Kotsk in which he advances the story of the Friday night incident as the clue to understanding why Menahem Mendel spent the last twenty years of his life in seclusion. He published another article, writing under the pseudonym of Y. Elzet,[9] entitled, "Kotsk" in *Ha-Mizrachi*, the publication of the Mizrachi movement in Poland, of which Slotnick was general secretary.[10]

---

4. Frenk, *Me-Hayyei ha-Hasidim,* 82. An interesting contemporary parallel occurs in M. Z. Feierberg's novella *Whither?*, where the hero grabs a lit candle on Yom Kippur and extinguishes it as a sign that he has lost his faith. Feierberg, *Whither? and Other Stories*, 125–26. I would like to thank Dr. Moshe Waldoks for this reference. An interesting Hasidic parallel is the case of Dov Ber of Leova, who tampered with a lit candle on the Sabbath as a sign that he had lost his faith. See, Horodetsky, *Hasidut ve-Hasidim*, 3:125. The possibility that Dov Ber of Leova was the historical inspiration for Frenk must be considered.

5. Heschel, *Kotsk,* 2:571.

6. E.g. "Rabbi Menahem Mendel . . . conducted his house in splendor and rode in a coach with a team of horses, as did the nobles of the land. Treasurers stood before his door to collect money from all who knocked at his door, and he traveled to other countries not for medical reasons, but to waste time in amusements and entertainments. (Yutzkin, "Pereq mi-Toldot ha-Hasidut be-Polonia," 340)"

7. On him see, Assaf, *The Regal Way,* Index, Dov Ber of Leova; Horodetsky, "Zaddiq she-Yaza le-Tarbut Ra'ah" in *Hasidut ve-Hasidim,* 3:124–54.

8. He used the pseudonym, L.Z. "Sihot u-Shemuot." *Reshumot* (Odessa) 1 (1918) 413–16. My thanks to Prof. David Assaf for bringing this source to my attention.

9. Chajes, *Ozar Biduyei ha-Shem* 35.538.

10. The article appeared simultaneously in *Ha-Ivri* (New York), the organ of the Mizrachi movement in America, under the title, "Le-Qorot ha-Hasidut R. Mendel mi-Kotsk."

Slotnick begins his article with a series of vignettes portraying R. Menahem Mendel as an ascetic scholar and thinker, unimpressed with miracles and unconcerned with material things. His only interests were study and the search for truth. Slotnick asserts that R. Menahem Mendel's two favorite books were Maimonides' *Guide for the Perplexed* and Ecclesiastes. Slotnick also mentions that after R. Menahem Mendel's death, Maimonides' treatise on logic [*Milot ha-Higayon*] with the commentary of Moses Mendelssohn was found in his bookcase. In the book was a notation that R. Menahem Mendel had taught this book to his children.

After these introductory sketches, Slotnick comes to the heart of his story. Detailing how Menahem Mendel was won over to the *Haskalah* and the resulting consequences, Slotnick relates that as his fame spread, he came to the attention of the contemporary *maskilim*. They decided to convince R. Menahem Mendel of their world-view, thus influencing the whole generation. To accomplish this goal, the *maskilim* selected one of their own, a dentist by profession, who settled in Kotsk near R. Menahem Mendel. News of this soon reached him and his curiosity was aroused. He had heard much about the *maskilim*, but had no personal experience with them.

One day R. Menahem Mendel complained of a toothache and ordered that the dentist be brought to him. The dentist came, examined him, and said that he would need to come to his house for treatment, as the necessary instruments were not portable. R. Menahem Mendel readily agreed and visited the dentist on a number of occasions. During these visits the dentist showed him the books in his library. He discussed their contents with him and lent them to him. R. Menahem Mendel had grown dissatisfied with the standard religious answers and had been searching for new solutions to the fundamental questions of life. Gradually, as his influence over R. Menahem Mendel grew, the dentist tried to convince him of his great responsibility to share his new insights with a wider audience. It was incumbent on R. Menahem Mendel to enlighten his followers. With one word he could show them the truth. The dentist argued that his sin would be very great if he failed in his duty. He urged R. Menahem Mendel to do something to publicly acknowledge his newly won truth.

The battle within R. Menahem Mendel raged fiercely. His family saw that he was disturbed but they had no idea what was wrong. They sent for his chief disciple, R. Mordecai Joseph of Izbica. He arrived in Kotsk on a Friday morning, but R. Menahem Mendel would not see him until the afternoon. When they met, R. Menahem Mendel suggested a walk in the neighboring woods. They walked for a while, silently immersed in their thoughts, smoking their pipes. Well into the forest, R. Menahem Mendel said, "How nice the world is. Let's sit and talk for a while."[11] R. Mordecai Joseph demurred, saying that it was late and the Sabbath was approaching. In fact, he did not want to enter into a conversation. R. Menahem Mendel fixed his gaze on him and his face grew dark, as did the sun, and they returned to town.

R. Menahem Mendel went to his room, where he remained during the prayers. Afterwards, the disciples gathered in the *bet midrash* and awaited R. Menahem Mendel's appearance. Shortly before midnight, he emerged from his room. He approached the table, and the goblet of wine was placed in his right hand. All eyes were on him. The battles between the archangel Michael and Satan raged on the battlefield of R. Menahem Mendel's soul. Suddenly, "what happened happened . . . the heart cannot reveal it to the mouth."[12] Pandemonium broke out, and many Hasidim tried to leave. Some even tried to escape through the windows. The only one to remain calm in this uproar was Mordecai Joseph. He announced in a loud voice: "Gentlemen, indeed "both the whole tablets and the broken tablets reside in the ark,"[13] but in a place where the name of God has been profaned one does not give honor to the master [*rav*]. He's lost his mind. Bind him."[14]

R. Mordecai Joseph immediately went into another room, where his followers prepared a table for him, and he began to act as a *rebbe*. At the conclusion of the Sabbath, R. Mordecai Joseph departed for Izbica, where he set up a Hasidic court. A large number of R. Menahem Mendel's Hasidim followed R. Mordecai Joseph to Izbica.

In a short time, R. Menahem Mendel calmed down and realized that nobody would listen to his ideas. He went into his room and remained there for the rest of his life. The Hasidim of Izbica and the *maskilim* of the generation spread the news that R. Menahem Mendel had become a heretic. Despite this, R. Isaac Meir of Gur and many Hasidim remained loyal to Menahem Mendel and did not leave Kotsk. This is the tale that Slotnick offered the readers of *Ha-Mizrachi*.

The publication of Slotnick's article generated a storm of indignation and controversy. Not only was he vehemently denounced, but a number

11. Slotnick, "Kotsk", 9.

12. Ibid. Slotnick, does not say what happened.

13. b. *Ber.* 8b.

14. Slotnick, "Kotsk", 9.

of leading rabbis urged that a ban of excommunication be issued against him for his defamation of R. Menahem Mendel of Kotsk.[15] Several issues later, *Ha-Mizrachi* published a rejoinder, entitled "Hizdiku et ha-*Zaddiq*," by Rabbi J. L Graubart, a close personal friend of Slotnick's and a co-worker in the Mizrachi movement.[16] Graubart questions what he sees as Slotnick's distortion of fact and his invention of traditions that have no factual basis. In addition, he briefly explains the intellectual basis of Menahem Mendel's teachings. His basic argument against Slotnick is based on the loyalty of the majority of Menahem Mendel's important followers, who were significant figures in their own right.[17] Graubart argues that they certainly knew the true facts, and it is inconceivable that they would have remained faithful to R. Menahem Mendel had he behaved as Slotnick described.

Two decades later, P. Z. Gliksman wrote *Der Kotsker Rebbe* to set the record straight and correct the inaccuracies and false legends surrounding R. Menahem Mendel of Kotsk.[18] Though primarily a Hebrew writer, Gliksman wrote this book in Yiddish in order to reach the widest possible audience.[19] He is primarily concerned with presenting an accurate picture of R. Menahem Mendel's life and teachings in his monograph. When he comes to the problem of the Friday night incident, he accepts the traditional Hasidic view that the incident never happened. He represents Slotnick as the villain of the drama and vehemently denies that there is any truth in his account. Gliksman underscores the implausibility of the family of R. Menahem Mendel sending for Mordecai Joseph. Hirsch of Tomaszow was R. Menahem Mendel's *shamash* (personal assistant) and lived in Kotsk. He would have been the natural person for the family to summon had anything been wrong.[20] Secondly, Gliksman notes that according to both Kotsker and Izbicer sources, R. Mordecai Joseph left Kotsk after *Simhat Torah* of

15. Gliksman, *Der Kotsker Rebbe* 61.

16. On the relationship between Graubart and Slotnick, see Graubart, "Rabbi Mendel Kotsker." Graubart is the son of J. L. Graubart. Unfortunately, he provides no new information on the Friday night incident or on Slotnick's motivations. My thanks to Mr. Zalman Alpert for this reference.

17. The only important disciple who left Kotsk with R. Mordecai Joseph was R. Leibele Eger of Lublin.

18. I have not been able to examine the articles written by S. Petrushka and H. Zeitlin during the interval between Slotnick and Gliksman (cited by Heschel, *Kotsk*, 2:671, nn. 2, 7, 9.

19. Gliksman, *Der Kotsker Rebbe* 6.

20. Ibid. 63.

5600 and not in 5599,[21] and strengthens his argument by introducing in evidence an important contemporary document, a letter written by R. Isaac Meir of Gur to R. Eliezer ha-Cohen of Poltuska. R. Eliezer had evidently heard that something was amiss in Kotsk and wrote to R. Isaac Meir in the spring of 1841 asking for clarification. R. Isaac Meir replied:

> I have just received your letter. This past Sabbath I was in Kotsk and, thank God, all is well. Three Sabbaths he [R. Menahem Mendel] sat with the gathering. The rumors no doubt emanated from accursed evildoers. In the city of Barzin, one rich man spoke ill [of R. Menahem Mendel] and the Hasidim acted appropriately. They made him pay a fine of 1,000 rubles. Thank God, nothing further was heard of the matter.[22]

The letter is important, but ambiguous. It shows that R. Isaac Meir denied strongly that anything unusual had happened in Kotsk. However, it also implicitly acknowledges that rumors were in the air about Kotsk and R. Menahem Mendel. Unfortunately, no other sources exist which might shed light on the origins or nature of these rumors.

Finally, Gliksman indicates that the story of R. Menahem Mendel's seclusion has been greatly exaggerated. He cites a wide variety evidence to show that he did not cut himself off from the world during his last twenty years. He did not hold public gatherings or grant audiences, as was customary for a *rebbe*, but he kept in close contact with events in both the Jewish community and the world at large. Gliksman quotes a number of letters written by R. Menahem Mendel during this period in which he comments on world events, and in one case offers advice on who should be appointed to a particular rabbinic position. He continued to see his close disciples regularly and spent every Sabbath afternoon examining his grandsons on their studies of the previous week. Gliksman paints a picture of R. Menahem Mendel in semi-seclusion, yet keeping a close watch on events around him.[23]

Both Graubart and Gliksman argue that Slotnick's story is implausible and contrary to all the available evidence. Additionally, they argue that were Slotnick's story true, it would have required a massive conspiracy

---

21. This is supported by Izbicer family tradition and the account in Leiner, *Dor Yesharim*, 30–33, which knows nothing of the Friday night incident.

22. Gliksman, *Der Kotsker Rebbe*, 59. The letter was originally published in Alter, *Meir Eynei ha-Golah*, para. 359.

23. Gliksman, *Der Kotsker Rebbe*, 63–67.

on the part of R. Menahem Mendel's followers to suppress the truth, and incredible loyalty and hypocrisy to remain attached to someone who had denied the most fundamental belief of Judaism. There is much merit in their argument. Slotnick's story is sufficiently suspect to be unacceptable as a historical account.

Joseph Opatoshu published his novel *In Poilishe Velder* shortly after the appearance of Slotnick's article.[24] Although written between 1915 and 1919, it is independent of Slotnick's work.[25] Opatoshu's book became one of the most popular and widely read Jewish novels in the interwar period. Its setting is Poland during the 1850s, and it includes a section on R. Menahem Mendel and the court in Kotsk. Opatoshu does not directly discuss the Friday night incident, but he does imply that R. Menahem Mendel's seclusion was not entirely voluntary. He writes in the novel:

> His intimates feared lest, with his interpretations of the Torah, the Rabbi [Menahem Mendel] might alienate the few remaining adherents. So they watched over him, and kept all strangers at a distance.[26]

Later in the same chapter, Opatoshu puts the following words into the mouth of a fictional character named "Barefoot Israel" who is half-mad and says things others would not dare say publicly. In a dramatic confrontation with R. Menahem Mendel, Israel says to him:

> Now is the time, Rabbi of Kotsk, for you to do penance! Your intellectual followers are selling their phylacteries. They say that this year leather has been very cheap in Kotsk. Such upstanding Jews as Hirsch Partzever and Hayyim Beer Grapitzer have taken an example from you, Rabbi, and agreed among themselves not to put on their phylacteries for three days. They wanted to see what effect this would have upon the order of the universe.[27]

The idea that there is something theologically amiss in Kotsk is further reinforced by the introduction of another fictional character named

---

24. The novel was published simultaneously in Yiddish and Hebrew. It was later translated into English as *In Polish Woods*. Quotations are from the English translation.

25. Reisen, *Leksikon fun der Yiddisher Literatur*, 1:148.

26. Opatoshu, *In Polish Woods*, 190.

27. Ibid., 202. Heschel, *Kotsk*, 2:659 n. 5, indicates that this story originally was published in Marcus, *Der Chassidismus*, 180. He also mentions that it was censored out of the later Hebrew translation of this book.

Daniel Eybeschutz.[28] He is supposed to be the son-in-law of R. Menahem Mendel's son, David.[29] Opatoshu portrays Daniel Eybeschutz as a follower of Sabbatai Sevi and Jacob Frank. The description of an orgy in Eybeschutz's house is reminiscent of stories regarding Jacob Frank and his followers.[30] Opatoshu leaves the reader with the impression that Kotsk in the 1850s was a hotbed of antinomianism. Menahem Mendel is depicted as having asked questions that opened a theological Pandora's box and ended up in antinomian heresy and orgies. The R. Menahem Mendel of the novel is a bitter and disillusioned figure who has withdrawn from the world, leaving a legacy of skepticism and antinomianism.

In Poilishe Velder was the literary sensation of the 1920s. It went through ten editions and was translated into six languages in the first decade after its appearance.[31] A central theme in most of the reviews of the novel is its historical accuracy. Secular reviewers generally accepted Opatoshu's portrayal of Menahem Mendel;[32] religious reviewers denounced it.[33] Even so eminent a historian as Meir Balaban devoted an article to the novel's historicity.[34] He judged it to be generally accurate but pointed out a few minor errors. Unfortunately, he passed over the section on R. Menahem Mendel in virtual silence.[35] The Hasidim of Poland did not remain silent, excommunicating Opatoshu and banning his novel.[36] In 1928 *In Poilishe*

28. The name is an allusion to Rabbi Jonathan Eybeschutz, who was accused of being a crypto-Sabbatian by Rabbi Jacob Emden. On Eybeschutz and Sabbatianism see, Perlmutter, *Jonathan Eybeschutz ve-Yahaso le-Shabtaut.*

29. For a list of David's real sons-in-law, see Gliksman, *Der Kotsker Rebbe,* 112.

30. Opatoshu, *In Polish Woods,* 268–92.

31. For a full listing of editions, translations, and reviews see, Shatzky, *Opatoshu Bibliographie.*

32. The comment of Koralnik, "Der Kotsker Nusach," is typical. He writes: "For me, Opatoshu's book is the first historical retelling about the Kotsker." The Joseph Opatoshu Collection in the YIVO Archives contains two scrapbooks in which Opatoshu collected the positive reviews.

33. An important negative review is that of H. Zeitlin, "Kotsker Hasidus un Modern Kunst Historisher Balaykhtung." Heschel cites this review as strongly supporting the negative position. *Kotsk,* 2:671 n. 9.

34. Balaban, "Di Historishe Motiven in Y. Opatoshu's In Poilishe Velder."

35. Balaban's only comment about Menahem Mendel is, "His enemies say that all is not well since 'that Sabbath' about which the Hasidim do not want to talk. (516)." Unfortunately he does not elaborate on this comment.

36. See, Kretsher, "Vegen Herem oif *Poilishe Velder.*" Margoshes, "Yidishe Cenzur (Vegen Herem)." I was not able to examine these articles.

Velder was made into a movie and its premier in Warsaw was the occasion of a riot by Hasidim.[37] Although Opatoshu does not mention the Friday night incident, a number of reviewers referred to it in a matter-of-fact way, as if it were common knowledge.[38]

There is no need to conjecture about Opatoshu's motives. His biographer, Nahman Meisel, quotes his public comments concerning the novel: "With Kotsk I wanted to describe the decay of Hasidism, the decline which comes from internal exhaustion, from its own depths."[39] Meisel observes, "It wasn't for nothing that this work so enraged the Hasidic pietists[40] in Poland that they excommunicated the author."[41]

Opatoshu intended his discussion of Hasidism in the novel to be polemical rather than a reflection of historical realities. Nonetheless, if the reviewers are a reliable indication, most readers saw it as historically valid. Opatoshu was less candid in an exchange of letters with P. Z. Gliksman during the same period. In his replies to the latter's strictures about the misrepresentations in the novel, Opatoshu argues that he is a novelist, not a historian, and must be allowed poetic license.[42] Surprisingly, Gliksman accepts Opatoshu's claim and does not consider the novel to be significant in the dissemination of the story of the "incident." Perhaps he thought fiction was not an influential medium.

In 1922 Martin Buber presented a different version of the Friday night incident in his book *Der Grosse Magid und Seine Nachfolger*.[43] According to Buber, the incident occurred at the third Sabbath meal (*seudah shelishit*). He further relates that R. Menahem Mendel rose and began to say that man is a part of God. Man has desires and lusts, and these too are part of God. The accounts differ, according to Buber, as to what else was said, but Menahem Mendel ended with the words: "There is no Law, and there is no Judge." Then he touched the candlesticks and left. R. Menahem Mendel

---

37. Z. Katz, "A Sensatsie Zevishen di Hasidim in Poilen Zulib a Muving Pictur."

38. Koralnik repeats the story of the antinomian act in his review. See above, n. 31. Jacobowitz, "A Roman fun Kotsker Hoif," remarks, "Various opinions are circulated about what happened. Some say that he was simply crazy, while others say that he said, 'There is no God.'"

39. Meisel, *Joseph Opatoshu*, 72.

40. He uses *frumakes*, a derogatory term.

41. Meisel, *Joseph Opatoshu*, 73.

42. Gliksman, *Der Kotsker Rebbe*, 70–73. Gliksman's letters to Opatoshu are preserved the Opatoshu Collection in the YIVO Archives.

43 Buber, *Grosse Magid*, xcv–xcvi.

remained in his room for thirteen years until his death.[44] During this time he would only extend his fingers through a crack in the door to greet visitors. Buber adds that this account is based on oral traditions.

Buber discusses the incident again in the revised version of *Der Grosse Magid, Tales of the Hasidim*. In the introduction to the second volume of the *Tales of the Hasidim*, he gives an entirely different account of the incident.[45] Employing Slotnick's story as the basis for the new version, he adds a few bits of color from his earlier account. Nevertheless, he still says that he is basing himself on oral reports. The debt to Slotnick is not acknowledged, nor is the radical disparity between the two versions accounted for.

Jiri Langer discusses Menahem Mendel briefly in his *Nine Gates*.[46] Recounting stories he heard at the court of Belz, he reports a legend that R. Menahem Mendel was spotted smoking on the Sabbath while on a visit to Lemberg (Lvov). Supposedly, the furor created in the aftermath of this incident drove R. Menahem Mendel into seclusion. Langer also mentions the story of the "enlightened" doctor, first found in Slotnick's article. *Nine Gates* does not contribute any new information, but it is an interesting illustration of the rumors and gossip that swirled around the memory of Menahem Mendel in other Hasidic courts as late as the 1930s.

In the post-World War II period, a number of scholars have touched on the Friday night incident. Menashe Unger in his novel, *Przysucha un Kotsk*, follows Slotnick with minor variations and contributes no new information. A. Z. Aescoli briefly mentions the incident without adding to our knowledge. He observes that many of the things ascribed to R. Menahem Mendel are taken from the life of R. Ber of Leova.[47] We have already seen an explicit example of this transposition.

Two biographies of R. Menahem Mendel by Isaac Alfasi and Joseph Fox were written from a religious apologetic perspective.[48] Following Gliksman, both deny the historicity of the Friday night incident. Fox adds a detail to the background of the story that renders reports of the incident

44. Buber confused the number of years Menahem Mendel acted as *rebbe* before his seclusion, thirteen (1827–39), with the number of years he was in seclusion, twenty (1839–59).

45. Buber, *Tales of the Hasidism*, 2:42–43.

46. Langer, *Nine Gates*, 256–61. *Nine Gates* was originally published in Czech in 1937. Langer was a *baal teshuvah* who became a Belzer Hasid. See, *Encyclopedia Judaica*, 10:1419-20. My thanks to Dr. Louis Jacobs for bringing this source to my attention.

47. Aescoli, *Ha-Hasidut be-Polin*, 2:124.

48. Alfasi, *Ha-Rabbi mi-Kotsk*; Fox, *Rabbi Menahem Mendel mi-Kotsk*.

more plausible. According to Fox's account, the Hasidic opponents of Kotsk spread rumors that the *Haskalah* had gained a foothold in Kotsk. This was so widely believed that Rabbi Jacob Orenstein, one of the most outspoken opponents of the *Haskalah*, was ready to ban marriages with Kotsker Hasidim.[49]

The most recent discussion of the incident is by A. J. Heschel in *Kotsk: Der Gerangel far Emesdikeit*. Heschel rejects Slotnick's account as completely groundless, observing that the image of R. Menahem Mendel in Slotnick's article is at odds with the image of Menahem Mendel in more reliable sources. Heschel adds several interesting new sources to the discussion that confirm his view that the stories of the "incident" have no factual basis. His first source is Alexander Zederbaum's *Keter Kehuna*. In this work, Zederbaum engages in very sharp polemics against Hasidism and writes about the crisis in Kotsk:

> In his last years a rumor spread that Anglican missionaries had talked to him [R. Menahem Mendel] and led him to heresy. Later it became known that this rumor was groundless. He was mentally ill and suffering from melancholia. This is why people were not allowed to see him.[50]

Another overlooked source cited by Heschel is the account of Hilary Nussbaum, a proponent of assimilation. Nussbaum mentions R. Menahem Mendel's isolation, but says nothing about his supposed heresy.[51] A third early source is Aaron Marcus, a Hasidic opponent of Kotsk. He does not mention the Friday night incident in his book on Hasidism.[52] Had he known of such an incident he would have surely used it to show the dangers of the Kotsker school of Hasidism.

In place of the Friday night incident, Heschel gives an entirely different explanation of the events leading up to R. Menahem Mendel's seclusion. According to an oral tradition, he suffered a nervous breakdown on the Sabbath of *parshat Toldot*, 5599 (1838). R. Menahem Mendel was ill during the whole winter and the following spring. The summer was spent recuperating and he was again ready to resume his public activities in time for *Rosh Hashanah*. R. Mordecai Joseph, who had been R. Menahem Mendel's

49. Fox, *Rabbi Menahem Mendel mi-Kotsk*, 55.

50. Zederbaum, *Keter Kehuna*, 132. Quoted in Heschel, *Kotsk*, 2:567.

51. Nussbaum, *Szkice Historyczne zZycia Zydow*, 127. Quoted in Heschel, *Kotsk*, 2:570.

52. Marcus, *Der Chassidismus*, 357.

closest disciple, differed with him on important issues. On the *Simhat Torah* of 5600 (1839), an incident occurred that precipitated the final break between R. Menahem Mendel and R. Mordecai Joseph. This was the beginning of the seclusion that lasted until the end of Menahem Mendel's life.[53] S. Petrushka, writing in Poland at the time of the Slotnick controversy, reported a similar tradition.[54] This version of R. Mordecai Joseph's departure from Kotsk is corroborated by H. S. Leiner, one of Mordecai Joseph's descendants, in the family history, *Dor Yesharim*.[55] Another of R. Mordecai Joseph's descendants, writing more recently, specifically denied that there was any truth to the story of the Friday night incident.[56]

The evidence of those who deny the historicity of the Friday night incident, particularly Gliksman and Heschel, far outweighs that of the proponents of its historicity. This still leaves the question of how the story started and why it attained such prominence. The Polish school of Hasidism was controversial, beginning with its inception in the dispute between the Yehudi of Przysucha and his teacher, the Seer of Lublin. Controversies between this school and other Hasidic schools continued to the end of the nineteenth century. R. Menahem Mendel's personality did nothing to mitigate the differences with other Hasidic groups. On the contrary, it only sharpened them. The readiness of R. Jacob Orenstein to believe that *Haskalah* had gained a foothold in Kotsk in 1838 shows the suspicion with which Kotsker Hasidim were viewed by other Hasidim.

Another aspect concerns undisputed events in R. Menahem Mendel's life: the nervous breakdown in 1838, the dispute with R. Mordecai Joseph of Izbica, and the twenty years of seclusion that followed. The dispute between the followers of Kotsk and Izbica continued for many years after R. Mordecai Joseph's departure from Kotsk. R. Isaac Meir's letter and the testimony of Alexander Zederbaum both indicate that contemporary rumors did circulate claiming some unholy occurrence in Kotsk.

A third aspect to be considered is the case of R. Ber of Leova, who in fact did the things ascribed to R. Menahem Mendel. At least one of the authors cited above, S. Y. Yutzkin, clearly confused R. Menahem Mendel with R. Ber of Leova. A. Z. Aescoli has also raised the possibility of mistaken identity. It is not unusual in the transmission of Hasidic legends for the

---

53. Heschel, *Kotsk*, 2:568–70.

54. Der *Haynt* (Warsaw), October 7, 1927. Quoted in Heschel, *Kotsk*, 2:570.

55. Leiner, *Dor Yesharim*, 33–34.

56. Leiner, *Tiferet Yeruchem*, 149–50.

deeds of a lesser known individual to be attributed to a well-known figure and vice versa.

Finally, the motives of those who disseminated this legend must be considered. A. N. Frenk was certainly no friend of the Hasidic movement. It may or may not be a coincidence that J. Slotnick was secretary of the *Mizrachi* movement in Poland and that the *Mizrachi* movement was involved in an acrimonious debate with the *Agudat Yisrael* party when he published his article. *Agudat Yisrael* was headed by the *rebbe* of Gur, who was considered by many the spiritual successor of Kotsk. In the case of Opatoshu, an avowed negative bias was shown. At the same time it must be remembered that the legend circulated orally independently of these authors. The references found in Opatoshu's reviewers indicate this.

The solution to the puzzle most probably lies in a combination of all these factors. The legend of the Friday night incident seems to have arisen from a convergence of R. Menahem Mendel's seclusion, the rumors circulating about the reasons for the seclusion, and R. Ber of Leova's embrace of *Haskalah*. An examination of all the available evidence shows that the legend of the Friday night incident has no real factual basis. How it came into existence and gained popularity remains a subject of speculation.

Appendix III: People Cited

Abraham of Sochaczew (1839–1910). Son-in-law of R. Menahem Mendel.

Abraham Joshua Heschel of Opatow (Apt) (1748–1825). Disciple of R. Elimelech of Lyzhansk and senior Hasidic figure in Galicia.

Akiva Eger (1761–1837). Famous Talmudic scholar and opponent of Hasidism. Grandfather of Leibele Eger.

Dov Ber (Maggid) of Mezhirech (1710–72). Successor of the Baal Shem Tov as leader of Hasidism.

Elimelech of Lyzhansk (1717–86). Disciple of R. Dov Ber (Maggid) of Mezhirech and teacher of the Seer of Lublin.

Hanokh of Aleksandrow (1798–1870). Disciple of R. Menahem Mendel.

Hirsch Parczewer. Disciple of R. Simhah Bunem and R. Menahem Mendel.

Hirsch Leib Kotsker. Disciple of R. Menahem Mendel.

Hirsch Tomaszower. Shamash, personal assistant, to R. Menahem Mendel.

Isaac of Warka (1779–1848). Disciple of R. Simhah Bunem and friend of R. Menahem Mendel.

Isaac Meir of Gur (1789–1866). Disciple of R. Simhah Bunem and R. Menahem Mendel. His closest disciple and founder of the Gur school of Hasidism, which became one of the most important Hasidic groups in Poland.

Israel Baal Shem Tov (1700–1760). The founder of Hasidism.

Israel (Maggid) of Kozienice (1733–1815). Disciple of Maggid of Mezhirech and important early Hasidic leader in Poland.

Jacob Arye of Radzymin (1792–1874). Disciple of R. Simhah Bunem and colleague of R. Isaac of Warka.

Jacob Isaac (Seer) of Lublin (1745–1815). The founder of Hasidism in Central Poland. The teacher of the Yehudi and R. Simhah Bunem of Przysucha.

Jacob Isaac (Yehudi) of Przysucha (1766–1813). Disciple of the Seer of Lublin and founder of the Przysucha school of Hasidism.

Joshua of Kutno (d. 1873). A Major Talmudic scholar of the period. Rabbi of Kutno.

Leibele Eger (1816–88). Grandson of R. Akiva Eger, disciple of R. Menahem Mendel and the most important disciple who left with R. Mordecai Joseph of Izbica, when he broke with Kotsk.

Levi Yitzhak of Berdichev (1740–1810). Disciple of R. Dov Baer of Mezhirech. Major figure of the third generation of Hasidism.

Mordecai Joseph of Izbica (1800–1854). Friend and disciple of R. Menahem Mendel. Broke with him in fall, 1839 and founded his own dynasty.

Moses Maimonides (1135–1204). The most important halakhic authority and philosopher of the Middle Ages.

Rashi (1040–1104). Acronym for R. Solomon ben Isaac, the author of the most important medieval commentary on Bible and Talmud.

Samuel Shmelke Horowitz of Nikolsburg (1725–78). Disciple of R. Dov Ber (Maggid) of Mezhirech and a founder of Hasidism in Poland.

Samuel of Shinove (d. 1873). Disciple of R. Simhah Bunem and R. Menahem Mendel. Author of *Ramatai'im Zofim*.

Samuel of Sochaczew (1855–1926). Grandson of R. Menahem Mendel. Author of *Shem mi-Shmuel* on the Torah.

Simhah Bunem of Przysucha (1765–1827). Disciple and successor of the Yehudi of Przysucha, teacher of R. Menahem Mendel of Kotsk and many others.

Solomon Leib of Leczna (d. 1843). Disciple of the Yehudi and R. Simhah Bunem of Przysucha. Yehiel Meir of Gostynin (d. 1888). Disciple of R. Menahem Mendel.

Yehudi. See, Jacob Isaac (Yehudi) of Przysucha.

Yerahmiel of Przysucha (1784–1839). Son of R. Jacob Isaac (Yehudi) of Przysucha.

Ze'ev Nahum of Biala (d. 1885). Father of R. Abraham of Sochaczew, the son-in-law of R. Menahem Mendel.

Ze'ev Wolf of Strykow (1806–91). Disciple of R. Menahem Mendel and R. Isaac Meir of Gur.

Zelig of Shrensk. Disciple of the Seer of Lublin and colleague of R. Simhah Bunem.

Appendix IV: Glossary

b.	Babylonian Talmud.
Bet Din.	A court based on Talmudic law.
Bet Midrash.	House of study, study hall. Also used as a synagogue.
Devekut.	Communion with God.
Gartel.	A black silk belt worn around the waist to separate the physical aspects of the person from his spiritual aspects.
Halakhah.	Jewish law.
Hametz.	Leavened products forbidden on Passover.
Hasid (pl. Hasidim).	Disciple of a *Zaddiq*. Member of a Hasidic community.
Humash.	The Torah, the five books of Moses.
Kavvanah.	Intention or concentration. Can also refer to Lurianic mystical meditations.
Kippah.	Skullcap, yarmulka.
Kvitel.	Lit. a note. A petition or request presented to a *zaddiq*.
m.	Mishnah.
Mikvah.	A ritual bath for immersion.
Mitnaged.	Lit. "opponent." Used as term for opponents of Hasidism.
Mitzvah.	Divine commandment, also can mean good deed.

Parshat.	Torah portion, section of the Torah read on a given week.
Pilpul.	Casuistic method of Talmud study popular in Eastern Europe. Also, an analysis of a Talmudic passage using this method.
Piyyut (pl. piyyutim).	Liturgical poems.
Pupik.	Lit. navel. Used in the sense of the gut, the emotions, as opposed to the intellect.
Rishonim.	Medieval scholars of Talmud and Rabbinic literature.
Rosh Hashanah.	Jewish New Year.
Simhat Torah.	The Festival of rejoicing with the Torah, at the end of *Sukkot*.
Sitra Achra.	The evil side. The forces of evil in Kabbalah.
Shamash.	Servant or personal assistant of an important person or a synagogue.
Shavuot.	Pentecost. Festival of giving of the Torah.
Shekhinah.	The presence of the Divine in the mundane world.
Shtreimel.	See *Spodek*.
Shulhan Arukh.	Code of Jewish law composed by R. Joseph Karo in the 16th century.
Spodek.	Polish style of fur hat worn by Hasidim on special occasions. *Shtreimel* is a different style of fur hat, worn by non-Polish Hasidim.
Sukkah.	The booth that is a central part of the festival of Sukkot [Tabernacles]. Jews eat in it for the first seven days of Sukkot.
Sukkot.	Festival of Tabernacles. Central rituals are eating or dwelling in the Sukkah and waving the *Lulav* and *Etrog*.
Talit.	A prayer shawl.

Tikkun Hazot.   Lurianic kabbalistic prayers recited in the middle of the night, mourning the destruction of the Temple and praying for the coming of the Messiah.

Ushpizin.   Seven shepherds of the Jewish people, symbolically invited into the sukkah, one each night.

Yom Kippur.   The Day of Atonement. The holiest day of the year.

Zaddiq (pl. Zaddiqim).   Righteous one; holy man. Master of a Hasidic community.

Bibliography

Aescoli, A. Z. *Ha-Hasidut be-Polin*. Edited by David Assaf. 2nd ed. Jerusalem: Magnes, 1999.

Alfasi, Yizhak. *Ha-Hoze Mi-Lublin*. Jerusalem: Mosad Harav Kook, 1969.

———. *Ha-Rabbi Mi-Kotsk*. Tel Aviv: Bitan Ha-Sefer, 1952.

Alter, A. Y. B. *Meir Eynei ha-Golah*. Brooklyn, NY: Tov, 1970.

Artan, Ya'akov Yisrael. *Emet ve-Emunah*. Jerusalem: Sphera, 1948.

Assaf, David. "Ha-Hasidut be-Hitpathuta-Diyukno shel R. Nehemiah Yehiel mi-Bychawa ben 'Yehudi ha-Kadosh." In *Ke-Minhag Ashkenaz U-Polin: Sefer Yovel le-Chone Shmeruk,* edited by Israel Bartal, et al., 269–98. Jerusalem: Merkaz Zalman Shazar, 1993.

———. "Veha-Mitnagedim Hitlozezu Shenishtaker ve-Nafal: Nefilato shel ha-Hoze mi-Lublin Beraei ha-Zikaron ha-Hasidi veha-Satira ha-Maskilit." In *Be-Ma'aglei Hasidim: Kovetz Mehkarim Mukdash le-Zikhro shel Mordecai Wilensky,* edited by Immanuel Etkes, et.al., 161–208. Jerusalem: Mosad Bialik, 1999.

———. *"Ne'ehaz be-Svakh": Pirkei Mashber u-Mabukhah be-Toldot ha-Hasidut*. Jerusalem: Merkaz Zalman Shazar, 2006.

———. *The Regal Way: The Life and Times of Rabbi Israel of Ruzhin*. Stanford: Stanford University Press, 2002.

Balaban, Maier. "Di Historishe Motiven in Y. Opatoshu's In Poilishe Velder." *Bichervelt* 6 (1922) 516–23.

Berger, Israel. *Simhat Israel*. Warsaw: Kleinman, 1910.

Berl, Hayyim Yehuda. *R. Abraham Joshua Heschel: Ha-Rav mi-Apta*. Jerusalem: Mosad Harav Kook, 1984.

Boim, Yehuda Menahem. *Rabbi Bunem mi-Przysucha*. 2 vols. Bnai Brak, Israel: Machon Torat Simhah, 1997.

Brill, Alan. "Grandeur and Humility in the Writings of R. Simhah Bunim of Przysucha." In *Hazon Nahum: Studies in Jewish Law, Thought and History Presented to Dr. Norman Lamm on the Occasion of his Seventieth Birthday,* edited by Yaakov Elman et al., 419–48. New York: Yeshiva University Press, 1997.

Bromberg, A. *Ha-Hoze Mi-Lublin*. Jerusalem: Machon Le-Hasidut, 1962.

Buber, Martin. *For the Sake of Heaven*. Philadelphia: Jewish Publication Society, 1953.

———. *Der Grosse Magid und Seine Nachfolger*. Frankfurt am Main: Rutten & Loening, 1922.

———. "Replies to My Critics." In *The Philosophy of Martin Buber,* edited by Paul Schilpp and Maurice Friedman, 731–41. Open Court: LaSalle, IL, 1967.

———. *Tales of the Hasidism*. 2 vols. New York: Schocken, 1947.

Chajes, S. *Ozar Biduyei ha-Shem*. Vienna: Glanz, 1933.

Dienstag, J. "Ha-More Nevuhim ve-Sefer ha-Mada be-Sifrut ha-Hasidut." In *Abraham Weiss Jubilee Volume*, 307–38. New York: Abraham Weiss Jubilee Committee, 1964.

Dynner, G. *Men of Silk: The Hasidic Conquest of Polish Jewish Society*. New York: Oxford University Press, 2006.

Elior, Rachel. "Between *Yesh* and *Ayin*: The Doctrine of the *Zaddik* in the Works of Jacob Isaac, the Seer of Lublin." In *Jewish History: Essays in Honour of Chimen Abramsky*, edited by Ada Rapoport-Albert and Steven Zipperstein, 393–455. London: Halban, 1988.

———. "Ha-Mahloqet al Moreshet Habad." *Tarbiz* 49 (1980) 166–86.

Encyclopedia Judaica. 16 vols. Jerusalem: Keter, 1971.

Etkes, Immanuel. *The Besht: Magician, Mystic, and Leader*. Waltham, MA: Brandeis University Press, 2005.

Faierstein, Morris M. *All Is in the Hands of Heaven: The Teachings of Rabbi Mordecai Joseph Leiner of Izbica*. Hoboken, NJ: Yeshiva University Press, 1989.

———. *All Is in the Hands of Heaven: The Teachings of Rabbi Mordecai Joseph Leiner of Izbica*. Rev. ed. Piscataway, NJ: Gorgias, 2005.

———. "The Friday Night Incident in Kotsk: History of a Legend." *Journal of Jewish Studies* 34 (1983) 179–89.

———. "Kotsk–Izbica Dispute: Theological or Personal?" *Kabbalah: Journal for the Study of Jewish Mystical Texts* 17 (2008) 75–79.

———. "*Personal Redemption in Hasidism*." In *Hasidism Reappraised*, edited by Ada Rapoport-Albert, 214–24. London: Littman Library of Jewish Civilization, 1996.

———. Review of, Abraham Joshua Heschel. *Kotsk: In Gerangel far Emesdikeit. Shofar*, 26 (2007) 211–14.

Feierberg, Mordecai Ze'ev. *Whither? and Other Stories*. Translated by Hillel Halkin. Philadelphia: Jewish Publication Society, 1972.

Fine, Lawrence. "The Art of Metoposcopy: A Study in Isaac Luria's Charismatic Knowledge." *AJS Review* 11 (1996) 79–101.

———. "'Tikkun': A Lurianic Motif in Contemporary Jewish Thought." In *From Ancient Israel to Modern Judaism: Essays in Honor of Marvin Fox*, edited by Jacob Neusner et al., 4:35–53. Atlanta: Scholars, 1989.

Fox, Joseph. *Rabbi Menahem Mendel mi-Kotsk*. Jerusalem: Mosad Harav Kook, 1967.

Frenk, Azriel N. *Me-Hayyei ha-Hasidim be-Polin*. In *Sifrei Agurah*, vol. 3, edited by Ben-Avigdor. 3 vols. Warsaw: Ben-Avigdor, 1896.

Gellman, Uriel. "The Great Wedding in Ustilag: Transmigrations of a Hasidic Myth [Hebrew]." *Tarbiz* 80 (2012) 567–94.

Gliksman, Pinchas Zelig. *Der Kotsker Rebbe*. Piotrikov, Poland: Landau, 1938.

Graubart, David. "Rabbi Mendel Kotsker." *Jewish Daily Forward*, October, 30, 1980.

Graubart, J. L. "Hizdiku et ha-Zaddiq." *Ha-Mizrachi* (Warsaw) 2.17 (1920) 7–8.

Heschel, Abraham Joshua. *Kotsk: In Gerangel far Emesdikeit*. 2 vols. Tel Aviv: Menorah, 1973.

———. *A Passion for Truth*. New York: Farrar, Straus & Giroux, 1973.

Horodetsky, Samuel Abba. *Hasidut ve-Hasidim*. 4 vols. Berlin: Dvir, 1923.

Jacobowitz, A. "A Roman fun Kotsker Hoif." *Haynt* (Warsaw), 1921.

Jacobs, Louis. *Their Heads in Heaven: Unfamiliar Aspects of Hasidism*. London: Vallentine Mitchell, 2005.

Katz, Steven T. "Martin Buber's Misuse of Hasidic Sources." In *Post Holocaust Dialogues: Critical Studies in Modern Jewish Thought*, 52–93. New York: New York University Press, 1983.

Katz, Zisha. "A Sensatsie Zevishen di Hasidim in Poilen Zulib a Muving Pictur." *Jewish Daily Forward*, April 12, 1929, 3.

Koralnik, A. "Der Kotsker Nusach." *Der Tog* (New York), May 29, 1921.

Kretsher, A. "Vegen Herem oif *Poilishe Velder.*" *Zeit* (New York), November, 1921.

Langer, Jiri. *Nine Gates*. Translated by S. Jolly. London: James Clarke, 1961.

Leiner, H. S. *Dor Yesharim*. Lublin, Poland: Sznajdermessara, 1925.

Leiner, Yeruchem. *Tiferet Yeruchem*. Brooklyn, NY: Machon Givaot Olam, 1948.

Levin, Judah Leib. *Ha-Admorim mi-Izbica*. Jerusalem: Nahliel, n.d.

Levinger, Ya'akov. "The Authentic Sayings of the Rabbi of Kotsk [Hebrew]." *Tarbiz* 55 (1986) 109–35.

————. "The Teachings of the Rabbi of Kotsk According to the Sayings Attributed to Him by His Grandson, R. Samuel of Sochaczew" [Hebrew]. *Tarbiz* 55 (1986) 413–31.

Liberman, Hayyim. "Legend and Truth about the Hasidic Printers [Yiddish]." *Ohel RH'L*. (Brooklyn) 2 (1980) 17–160.

Mahler, Raphael. *Hasidism and the Jewish Enlightenment*. Philadelphia: Jewish Publication Society, 1985.

Malak, Z. Y. *Abir ha-Ro'im*. Piotrikov, Poland: Falman, 1935.

Marcus, Aron. *Der Chassidismus*. Pleschen, Poland: Verlag des Jeschurun, 1901.

Margoshes, Joseph. "Yidishe Cenzur (Vegen Herem)." *Zeit* (New York), December 19, 1921.

Meisel, Nachman. *Joseph Opatoshu: Sein Leben und Werk*. Warsaw: Literarishe Bletter, 1937.

Morgenstern, Aryeh. "Messianic Expectations and the Settlement in Israel in the First Half of the Nineteenth Century [Hebrew]." *Cathedra* 24 (1982) 52–78.

————. "Messianic Expectations for the year 5600 (1840) [Hebrew]." In *Messianism and Eschatology* [Hebrew], edited by Z. Baras, 343–64. Jerusalem: Merkaz Zalman Shazar, 1992.

Nigal, Gedalya. *The Hasidic Tale*. Oxford: Littman Library of Jewish Civilization, 2008.

Nussbaum, Hilary. *Szkice Historyczne z Zycia Zydow w Warszawie*. Warsaw: Kowalewskiego, 1881.

Opatoshu, Joseph. *In Polish Woods*. Translated by Isaac Goldberg. Philadelphia: Jewish Publication Society, 1938.

Perlmutter, M. A. R. *Jonathan Eybeschutz ve-Yahaso le-Shabtaut*. Jerusalem: Schocken, 1947.

Piekarsz, Mendel. *Bein Ideologia le-Meziut*. Jerusalem: Mosad Bialik, 1994.

————. *Ha-Hanhagah ha-Hasidit*. Jerusalem: Mosad Bialik, 1999.

————. "'The Inner Point' of the *Admorim* of Gur and Aleksandrow as a Reflection of their Ability to Adjust to Changing Times. [Hebrew]" In *Studies in Jewish Mysticism, Philosophy and Ethical Literature: Presented to Isaiah Tishby*, edited by Joseph Dan et al., 617–60. Jerusalem: Magnes, 1986.

Rabinowicz, Zvi Meir. *Rabbi Simhah Bunem mi-Przysucha*. Tel Aviv: Mosad Harav Kook, 1945.

————. *Rabbi Yaakov Yizhak mi-Przysucha: ha-Yehudi ha-Qadosh*. Piotrikov, 1932.

Rakatz, Y. Y. K. *Siah Sarfei Kodesh*. Lodz, Poland: Mesorah, 1926. Reprint. 5 vols. in 1. n.p., n.d.

Rapoport-Albert, Ada. "God and the Zaddik as the Two Focal Points of Hasidic Worship." *History of Religions* 18 (1979) 296–325.

Reisen, Zalman. *Leksikon fun der Yiddisher Literatur, Presse, un Filologie.* 4 vols. Vilna, Lithuania: Vilner Verlag, 1925–28.

Rosen, Michael. *The Quest for Authenticity: The Thought of Reb Simhah Bunim.* Jerusalem: Urim, 2008.

Rosman, Moshe. *Founder of Hasidism: A Quest for the Historical Baʾal Shem Tov.* Berkeley: University of California Press, 1996.

Sack, Bracha. "Iyyun be-Torato shel ha-Hoze mi-Lublin." In *Zaddiqim ve-Anshei Maʾase,* edited by Israel Bartal, et al., 219–39. Jerusalem: Mosad Bialik, 1994.

Scholem, Gershom. "Martin Buber's Interpretation of Hasidism." In *The Messianic Idea in Judaism and Other Essays on Jewish Spirituality,* 227–50. New York: Schocken, 1971.

Shapira, Abraham. "Shtei Darkei Geulah be-Hasidut be-Aspeklaria shel Martin Buber." In *Massuʾot: Mekhkarim be-Sifrut ha-Kabbalah ube-Mahshevet Yisrael Mukdashim le-Zikhro shel Prof. Ephraim Gottlieb z'l,* edited by Michal Oron et al., 429–46. Tel Aviv: Mosad Bialik and Tel Aviv University, 1994.

Shatzky, Jacob. *Opatoshu Bibliographie.* New York: Workmen's Circle, 1937.

Sherwin, Byron L. *Mystical Theology and Social Dissent: The Life and Works of Judah Leowe of Prague.* London: Littman Library of Jewish Civilization, 1982.

Singer, Isaac B. *Satan in Goray.* New York: Noonday, 1955.

Shinove, Samuel of. *Ramatai'im Zofim.* Jerusalem: Lewin-Epstein, 1978.

Slotnick, Judah L. "Kotsk." *Ha-Mizrachi* (Warsaw) 2.14 (1920) 7–10.

———. "Le-Qorot ha-Hasidut R. Mendel mi-Kotsk." *Ha-Ivri* (New York) 10.19 (1920) 9–12.

———. "Sihot u-Shemuot." *Reshumot* (Odessa) 1 (1918) 413–16.

Sochaczew, Samuel of. *Shem Mi-Shmuel.* 9 vols. Piotrikov, Poland: Falman, 1929–34.

Unger, Menashe. *A Fire Burns in Kotsk: A Tale of Hasidism in the Kingdom of Poland.* Translated by Jonathan Boyarin. Detroit: Wayne State University Press, 2015.

Walden, Aaron. *Kol Simhah.* Breslau, Poland: Hirsh Sulzbach, 1859.

Werses, Shmuel. "Ha-Hasidut be-Aspeklaria Belletristit: Iyyunim be-Gog U-Magog shel Martin Buber." In *Zaddiqim ve-Anshei Maʾase,* edited by Israel Bartal et al., 317–56. Jerusalem: Mosad Bialik, 1994.

Wiesel, Elie. *Souls on Fire.* New York: Random House, 1972.

Yaari, Abraham. *Toldot Hag Simhat Torah.* Jerusalem: Mosad Harav Kook, 1954.

Yadimowa, Yehiel Moshe of. *Likkutim Hadashim.* Ashdod: Moshe Blotnick, 2003.

———. *Niflaot Hadashot.* Ashdod: Moshe Blotnick, 2003.

Yutzkin, S. Y. "Pereq mi-Toldot ha-Hasidut be-Polonia." In *Nahum Sokolow Jubilee Volume,* 335–40. Warsaw: Bnei Zion, 1904.

Zederbaum, Alexander. *Keter Kehuna.* Odessa: A. Zederbaum, 1866.

Zeitlin, Hillel. "Kotsker Hasidus un Modern Kunst Historisher Balaykhtung." *Moment* (Warsaw), August 19, 1921.

Zigelman, E. Z. *Ohel Torah.* New York: Bet Hillel, 1984.